Is There Hope for the City?

Biblical Perspectives on Current Issues

Howard Clark Kee, General Editor

IS THERE HOPE
FOR THE CITY?

Donald W. Shriver, Jr.
and Karl A. Ostrom

W
The Westminster Press
Philadelphia

Scripture quotations are from *The New English Bible* © The Delegates of the Oxford University Press and The Syndics of the Cambridge University Press, 1961, 1970, and are used by permission.

First edition

Published by The Westminster Press ®
Philadelphia, Pennsylvania

Printed in the United States of America

9 8 7 6 5 4 3 2 1

Library of Congress Cataloging in Publication Data

Shriver, Donald W.
  Is there hope for the city?

  (Biblical perspectives on current issues)
  Includes bibliographical references and index.
  1. Cities and towns—Biblical teaching.
I. Ostrom, Karl A   1939–   , joint
author. II. Title III. Series.
BS680.C5084   220.8'301'363   77–22187
ISBN 0–664–24147–6

To
PEGGY LEU SHRIVER
AND CAROLYN MONTGOMERY OSTROM
JAMES LUTHER ADAMS
AND ROBERT N. BELLAH
who have often given us
courage to hope for
a Better City

Contents

Editor's Preface

No other aspect of modern life more accurately reflects the heights of technical achievement and the depths of human tragedy than our cities. In the Bible the city serves as symbol both of man's evil determination to live in independence of God (Gen. 11:4) and of the hope that God will achieve his purpose for his people (Rev. 21:10). Elsewhere in Scripture the People of God are represented as a city, the object of God's love. The Good News Bible translates Isa. 62:12, "You will be called 'God's Holy People' . . . 'The City That God Loves.'"

In the eighteenth and nineteenth centuries, the skylines of American cities were dominated by church spires. Today both spires and religious institutions seem to be eclipsed or replaced by commercial enterprises. The flight to the suburbs of the middle class either has been matched by the churches or has left behind echoing monuments to a seemingly irrecoverable past.

Recently our society has been seeking ways to revitalize its cities, to lure dwellers and shoppers back, to renew historically and architecturally appealing sections of downtown areas. But the unmet needs of those who never left the city as well as of those who are now returning will never be supplied by glittering urban malls and shopping galleries or by pocket parks. Neither will they be met by a church that does no more than repeat the compassionate words of Frank Mason North:

> In haunts of wretchedness and need,
>   On shadowed thresholds dark with fears,
> From paths where hide the lures of greed
>   We catch the vision of Thy tears.

. . . .
O Master, from the mountain side,
   Make haste to heal these hearts of pain;
Among these restless throngs abide,
   O tread the city's streets again.

Rather, what is required is a perspective, based on Biblical insight and empirical analysis, of what is the potential of the church in the city to effect redemptive change in human lives and in social structures.

The authors of this book embody the qualities and capabilities that are requisite for providing insight and proposing lines of action on this issue. Donald Shriver has given dramatic statement to his personal commitment to the church in the city by accepting the presidency of Union Theological Seminary in New York City. That institution is surrounded by the challenge through its proximity to a major cluster of academic institutions, to the upper West Side mixture of the poor, the artists, the professionals, the academics, and to festering Harlem. Overshadowing Union to the west are the soaring towers of Riverside Church and the Interchurch Center. How relevant to the city's needs is this aggregation of academic and ecclesiastical institutions? Donald Shriver has been joined in his search for answers concerning the church's role in the city by Karl Ostrom, a social scientist and clinical psychologist with theological training. Dr. Ostrom is skilled in assembling and analyzing empirical evidence, which is an indispensable safeguard against either wishful thinking or unwarranted despair.

Written with keen insight and profound compassion, this demanding, illuminating book offers a timely message to the church and its leadership, both lay and clerical, concerning the untapped potential for serving as a channel of grace in our cities. The church can rise to that challenge only when it finds ways to enable urban dwellers to look "forward to the city with foundations, whose architect and builder is God" (Heb. 11:10).

HOWARD CLARK KEE

Bryn Mawr, Pennsylvania

Chapter 1

An Array
of Hopes and Fears

A book about Biblical faith and modern urban society calls for some explaining. Why the Bible? And why the Bible's connection with modern urban society?

We can begin to answer the first question by pairing it with another posed not long ago by the eminent biologist, Lewis Thomas. Imagine that our radio telescopes have received a communication from planetary creatures in a star system one hundred light-years from earth. What message would we choose to beam back to them? The information we send, he cautions, will have to be of interest to us *two hundred* years from now, because when the next step in this interstellar conversation occurs, that many years will have passed. "We would have to choose with durability of meaning in mind," which would eliminate most current scientific theories and virtually all the news in our daily newspapers. My vote, says Thomas, would be

> for Bach, all of Bach, streamed out into space, over and over again. We would be bragging, of course, but it is surely excusable for us to put the best possible face on at the beginning of such an acquaintance.[1]

Human beings differ widely on what they consider to be their "best possible face." It is a question of what one values most in the human enterprise. Here the authors wish to side with Thomas, not only in choosing the message of Bach, but in choosing what lies behind much of Bach: the message of the Bible. How could anyone decipher the choral music of Bach without some comprehension of the messages in human history from a certain Abraham, Jeremiah, Jesus, and Paul?

John Calvin used to say that the Bible is the "spectacles" by which

Christians look at everything around them. The Bible provides *perspective*, an angle of vision, for seeing the world. But no human being can look at everything at once. We have to focus on something that, presumably, we want to see. In this book, the two authors are seeking to focus, through the perspective of the Bible, upon the challenges and problems of human relationships in the cities of America. Suppose we introduce our focus on modern urban society by introducing six particular persons in that society. These six enter our field of vision as typical of the human neighborhood that will concern us in this book. We will meet all six, from time to time, on other pages.

1. Shirley Weatherford lives in a suburban community of Atlanta. In 1975 she almost died there. One Sunday morning, while reading the newspaper in bed, she collapsed and stopped breathing, the victim of cardiac fibrillation. Luckily her husband was at hand. He reached for the telephone and called the mobile emergency squad of the county hospital. A daughter, at home from college, cried out, "Try mouth-to-mouth resuscitation!" Five minutes later, the emergency crew arrived. As they took her to the hospital, the doctor on duty radioed treatment instructions to the ambulance. "If she had lacked either the mouth-to-mouth or the emergency unit," he said later, "she would be dead."

A few weeks later, recovering, she and her family asked themselves anxiously, "Suppose we had lived in a county without an emergency squad?"

2. Harrisene Little was born in 1941 in The Bronx, one of four children of a mother on welfare. "I remember that awful-tasting oatmeal that was stamped, 'Not to be Sold, Gov't Property, Welfare Recipients Only.'" Six years later her mother, age twenty-six, was murdered. The next twenty years of Harrisene's life consisted largely in a struggle to survive economically while she tried also to become formally educated. "From the time I was a child I promised my unborn children that they would never hunger for the basic needs in life, which every parent owes their offspring—food, good shoes, books, knowledge, and most of all, understanding." After ten years in three New York schools, she married at fifteen. At twenty-two she had three children.

In 1967 she wrote a letter to an official of the City College of New York to declare her hope of passing the qualifying test for admission to the college. Toward the end of the letter she said:

"I've had nine jobs in the past four years. Struggling to produce three productive citizens who are a credit to their country and their world. Not just to exist and become burdens on my society. But I need help. . . .

". . . [The children's] father is in Vietnam. He'll be stationed in the Far East for three years. He never had much interest in them anyway. Thus, it is up to me, I am their tree, they are my branches. I must not fall or fail them.

"These are some of the reasons why I've got to go back to school; in paving a future for myself it will be for them. I'm scared, not just afraid. I must be qualified. I must get a degree, in order to survive; otherwise I might just as well throw in the towel. . . .

"I'd like to be a teacher in any poverty-stricken area to help children and teach them and most of all give them hope. . . . I'm studying very hard. I haven't fallen asleep over school books in eleven years. I'm going to make a good mark on my test in March; when I get the results I'll send them to you."[2]

3. Philip Delaney drives thirteen miles to work every morning. He crosses the Golden Gate bridge, which for him is the most beautiful entrance to the most beautiful city in the world—San Francisco. After years of training in both law and business schools in Berkeley, he finds himself a vice-president in the International Division of the largest bank in the United States. Fresh from a southern California college in 1950, he "discovered" Asia by landing as a second lieutenant in the U.S. infantry that invaded South Korea's Inchon Peninsula. The Korean war left him convinced that law and finance were superior to missiles and armies as bridges across the Pacific. As he drives across the Golden Gate on some foggy mornings, he even imagines that bridge-building is what international trade is all about.

Since 1970, however, his confidence in himself as a successful professional in a great business institution in a great city has been somewhat shaken—chiefly through his children. That was the year two of them almost left home. His son Bill was seventeen that spring. Right after the Kent State "massacre" he announced one suppertime that he was bound for Vancouver. His daughter Lucy, a high school sophomore, looked across the table on that same evening and delivered herself of this devastation:

"Look, Dad, you sit in your bank all day and make loans to straw hat manufacturers in Hong Kong, while a few miles away people like Bill are getting killed just like you almost got killed in Korea—for what? Down the hall of your bank somebody else is probably making more loans for landfill to put more apartments and restaurants out into San Francisco Bay—for what? People are dying from the pollution our two cars help to put into the air around this city—for what? Your bank makes money out of junk in this country just to loan it to people to make more junk in Asia! It all seems so pointless. A big noisy merry-go-round. Sometimes I wish I hadn't been born in this country. My high school counselor actually had the nerve to tell us the other day that freeway construction would be a 'growth industry' in California for many years to come. She wanted us to 'prepare for our futures.' What a terrific future: paving over some more of California! And your own father's bank paying lots of taxes to buy the concrete!"

Whatever replies Philip had to this went unremembered for the next few years. It was the beginning of his awareness that the time was overdue for him to do some thinking about her simple question: "For what?" It embarrassed him that he had no ready answers. Such answers as he had sounded uncertain, fuzzy. It used to be that in riding into San Francisco he had at least a vague feeling of personal significance. Now he wasn't so sure. Nor were lots of his friends at the Executive Club. Were they all emperors without clothes?

4. "I can't understand why he doesn't play with the other five-year-olds on the block," said Louella McCabe to her husband, Thomas. "He just sits on the steps all bleary-eyed. And the only time he smiles is throwing a tin can at somebody. I don't know what to do with him. He's supposed to go to school next year. I'm scared that they won't let him enter first grade."

Tom's shoulders shrugged and sagged. "Try the City Hospital."

"How can I do that? You take a whole day off from work, and then you get told to come back next week. Last time it took me two buses and one taxi to get there, and you had to *shove* your way into that clinic. The doctor talks with you so fast that you figure he doesn't really want to know what you know about your own child. That place doesn't cure people; it makes them sick."

"Take him anyway," said Tom, as he turned on the television.

So she took off the next Thursday, losing twenty-four dollars by not going to work. She waited in line for three and a half hours in the room where all the paint was peeling from the ceiling.

"Boston is supposed to get a new City Hospital," said the lady jammed beside Louella. "There's no money from Washington." But the first word from the intern, when she finally took Tommy into the office, was cheerful: "You're in luck, Mrs. McCabe. Take him right up to room 105, where they are about to administer the weekly diagnostic tests for children. You picked the right day to come."

"Oh," she said, and took Tommy to room 105.

It was four thirty when the lady with tinted glasses said to the fifteen parents in the waiting room: "We're all finished with the children now. You will get a letter in the mail telling you the results of the test; and you can come back to discuss the results with one of the clinic doctors."

The last to leave, Louella turned to the lady with a half smile: "I've been so worried about my boy. Can't you tell me a little bit about the results of the test?"

"I'm sorry, no. But you'll get the letter before the month is over."

As the door shut behind her, the lady in the glasses said to the black man stuffing folders into the filing cabinet: "The truth is that I'm glad not to tell that woman the results of the test. That little boy was malnourished before he was born. He has the mental age of a two-year-old, and I'll bet he never goes to public school. She'll have no money to hire a sitter to take care of him, and the Lord only knows where he'll end up."

"His big mistake," said the man, slamming the file drawer shut, "was being born black in Roxbury. It was all over with him before he saw the light of day. Everything we do for him in this hospital will add up to a Band-Aid. It makes you tired to come to work in the morning . . . mighty tired." But his associate didn't answer. She was looking out the window at Louella McCabe holding Tommy's hand at the bus stop.

5. Believing that government was both the problem and the hope of the American people, Paul Ransom took the job offered him in the Department of Health, Education, and Welfare in Washington: Deputy Assistant Secretary for Field Management and Policy Development. What did that mean? If asked at a cocktail party, he could have given a rational answer; but, as it happened, his mind gave him a nonrational answer, as minds have a way of doing, in a dream.

"I had worked at my job in Washington for several months," he said. "The 'stuff' of the dream came straight out of my on-the-job training. I found myself in a large space, somewhat bewildered and in need of assistance. Before me at a hazy distance was a vast bank of cubbyholes, reminiscent of the old Horn & Hardart automat. I had the strong sense that in those cubbyholes lay a large number of things which I needed.

"Between me and the bank of goodies, I saw a line of turnstiles; and beyond the turnstiles, long alleys with high walls bent this way and that, like a maze. With my eyes on the cubbyholes, I went through a turnstile and worked my way down one of the alleys, somehow assured that I knew the way. After a long time, I finally reached my goal: a cubbyhole with a handle. Turning the handle, I found it locked. In utter frustration, I pulled at this and that cubbyhole, only to find all of them locked. Then I noticed on the far left-hand wall another bank—a bank of keys! The thought swept over me: If only I knew which key fitted which cubbyhole, I might get any one of them open! And then I woke up: as if the job of discovering how all those keys matched all those locks was too much dreamwork for one night. During my waking-work at HEW the next few days, I was troubled with some haunting questions: If even the experienced bureaucrat has trouble fitting the right key to the right bureaucratic service slot, what about the ordinary American citizen? What is the good of knowing how to get through the turnstiles and the mazes of the bureaucracy if the last door is going to be locked anyway? Where is the key that unlocks the help which *somebody* in this society has the power to give me?"

When he related his dream to the authors of this book, he had left government service for the university. But he is no more certain now that the university has the answer to the questions than he was certain about government. Informed by us that we expected to use his dream as part of this book, he exclaimed: "Hurry! There is not much time to change the behavior that will save this planet!"

6. Born in 1955 on a hillside farm ninety miles north of Mexico City, Luis Fernández knew from an early age that his permanent home would probably not be that hillside farm. He was the sixth of seven children. Before he was twelve years old, three of his older brothers had left for jobs in the city. Five years later, the time seemed right for Luis to make the same trek south. Just then a letter arrived from Juan, his oldest brother: "Tell Luis that the jobs in Mexico City are so scarce and so cheap that my advice is to try over the border. I see thousands of young men out of work and on the streets here every day. It won't hurt him to try San Antonio. I hear they need hand labor to line irrigation ditches, and right now they are hiring people without a lot of checking with Immigration. If he can stay on the farm, that would be best. If he can't, I'd hate to see him swallowed up here." The response to the letter by his father and mother was a long, long discussion, his mother pleading, "He's needed to tend the corn," and his father shaking his head, "He's needed to make some money."

Luis finally decided to end the argument. He disappeared one morning before sunrise, leaving behind a note saying, "I'll be back in a few months with some dollars!" He felt proud making that decision. He felt sure that his father was proud of him too.

How he got to San Antonio, he later preferred not to remember. It was a long trip; he was often hungry. He eluded many uniformed officials; he learned many English phrases. Finally, he stood so long in the "Job Application" line, that the end of the journey was the only part he really wanted to remember. But even that was not pleasant. An unshaven white man behind him in the line said angrily to the man at the employment office desk: "Listen here, this little Mexican kid is up here looking for a job without a work permit. I've got an eighteen-year-old son looking for a job in Houston, and he can't find one. If you hire him, I'm goin' right to Immigration. Nobody's goin' to hire them wetbacks over my own children. It's gettin' so that real Americans don't count anymore. But me and my children *are* goin' to count, see?"

Luis did not understand all of this, but he understood the shaking of the head of the man behind the desk. And he understood what the fellow Mexican said to him outside the office: "You are a courageous young man, my friend; but you must be the one thousandth young Mexican to show up here in the past month. Count yourself lucky that the company agent did not take down your name and turn it over to the officials. The jobs are here, all right, but everybody from the Governor to the Congressman to the Mayor to the police are being pressured to hold every job open for a 'real American.' They'll come all the way from New York City to get these jobs in San Antone, and they'll say that nobody living south of the Great River can get them. If there's any corn to eat on your farm, Luis, go back there. The Yankees used to want you here to do their dirty work. But now they don't even want you for that. They'll make you feel like a hunted animal if you stay. Even Mexico City might be better! Or maybe, no city at all."

A COLLISION OF DREAMS

There is a danger starting this book that way. It is the danger of television.

Like glimpses into the joys and sorrows of the people who frequent the six o'clock news, the soap operas, and the weekly dramas, here they are: Shirley Weatherford, Harrisene Little, Philip Delaney, Louella McCabe, Paul Ransom, Luis Fernández, and others who are the human reality about whom this book is written. We have looked in on their lives a bit, and we have the option now of deciding if such lives interest us enough to follow them any farther. Another channel, maybe? . . . And there's the danger: *to perceive such people merely as items of information and not as our neighbors.* In a curious, troubling way, the tube has permitted many moderns to look in *on* one another without having to look out *for* one another. That is the target-evil against which this book is directed, against which much of the Bible is directed too.

An astute analyst of the influence of television on American life puts it this way:

The unique excellence of television is also its tragic flaw. It captures the present only to become a captive of the present. With a childlike sense of wonder at the flashing moment, it is plagued with a child's short attention span. . . .

The artistic device of television is synecdoche. The part stands for the whole, because the part can be seen in an image, whereas the whole has to be envisioned in the larger intellectual reaches of consciousness.

We see a boy throwing a rock at a tank in Ulster, but have no sense of the centuries of conflict in Ireland. We see a soldier lighting a thatched hut in Vietnam, a black man bleeding on a street in Watts, and a line of men and women waiting for work. What it all means, no one can say.[3]

Human beings, this author goes on to say, seem to get around eventually to some assertions about "what it all means." The persons whom we have just met provide good examples. Harrisene Little understands her life as a struggle to achieve what her society calls a formal education. She wants to return to the ghetto to assist others into the same achievement. As she projects it, that is an outline of her life story. Paul Ransom dreams of a human world in which the help that some people have to provide other people is facilitated through institutions. His is a life story largely frustrated. Philip Delaney started his career believing that he might play a part in building world peace through law and commerce. For him, middle age is becoming a time of great anxiety; the dream, the image by which he organized the meaning of his life as a young man, no longer seems to "work." His children question his answers to the question, "For what?" Even if he succeeded in clearly verbalizing them, the answers would be psychologically threatened by certain facts in his life— beginning with the facts of his children's opinions.

We believe that human beings *can* say what it all means. Eventually they must say so, else their personal integrity and their social vocations go to pieces. An eloquent testimony to this same belief appears in a recent book, *Faith After the Holocaust,* by the Jewish scholar, Eliezer Berkovits. Our common human position, he says, is that of Tarrou, a character in Albert Camus's novel, *The Plague.* Along with his friend, Dr. Rieux, Tarrou commits himself to the alleviation of suffering among the plague-stricken citizens of his city. "All he understands is that there are pestilences on this earth and there are victims. And it is up to us, so far as possible, not to join forces with the pestilences. Of this he says: 'I know it's true.' But how does he know?" Why be concerned at all with the victims of plague or any other source of human pain? The two friends discuss the problem without finding an answer. "Really it's too damn silly living in and for the plague. Of course a man should fight for the victims, but if he ceases caring for anything outside that, what's the use of the fighting?" And so, comments Berkovits,

> to prove to themselves that they do care for something outside that, they go for a swim. At first this may seem rather opaque, until we learn to understand the symbolic significance of the swim. For in order to be able to swim, one has to leave the town; one has to pass through the closely guarded gates of the city of the plague; one must have special passes. Finally, far out in the fresh water of the bay one is "at last free of the town and the plague." The town with its pestilence is the symbol of the absurdity of existence, and the fight for the victims is the meaning introduced into this absurdity by man. It is the attempt to be a saint without God. But it is not enough; it does not work. One has to go for a swim in the bay, outside the gates of this absurdity. The swim symbolizes the need for the beyond, for a transcendental value reference.[4]

To cultivate and explore meanings deep and comprehensive enough to give some sense to everything in our lives is the principal business of religion. The origins of the Latin term *religio* are not very clear, but one translation of the word is, "bind together." Paul Tillich used to say that the religion of persons and societies is their "ultimate concern." Or as some more recent theologians might put it: *Religion is a story about the whole world that gives the storyteller a time, a place, and a role in it.*

It is no secret that late-twentieth-century life poses some great difficulties for religion so defined. Where, in the booming, buzzing confusion of our complex global civilization is there a story that really "gets it all together"? Anthropologists tell us sorrowfully about the destruction of ancient Indian cultures by the aggressions of the Europeans on the American continent. Prior to the white man's coming, Indians could locate themselves in a territory, in a social organization, and around a set of ceremonies that bound their life into an understandable, whole pattern. Whites and Indians met each other in America in a collision of dreams. The deepest of their conflicts was religion; they lived and moved by different ultimate concerns. This is just one illustration among hundreds that might be selected to image one of the terrors of life for people white, red, black, brown, and yellow in today's world. We have a growing stock of information about each other but few religious certainties that bind us together as mutually affirming neighbors. Perhaps the illustration on the largest scale is the phenomenon of our *cities*.

A decade ago Marshall McLuhan said that the planet earth was becoming a "global village," a worldwide society interconnected by radio, telephone, and television. How little mere technology means in binding people together, however, becomes immediately apparent to any person in a large American city who flips through one of those three-inch-thick telephone books. Of all those people whom would I ever *think* of calling? How very few do I *want* to call me! Apartments in the big cities are sometimes compared to beehives, but the comparison is inaccurate. A beehive is an insect community. Human apartment dwellers meet in halls and elevators, but night and day they hardly think of each other. What binds them together most frequently is probably their access to the same local television channels. The bigger the city the more diversity of human types; and the more determined people are to say to outsiders: "Leave us alone!" Large cities offer many examples of what one sociologist called urban villagers—groups of people who seldom stray outside the few blocks where they live, and who perceive the rest of the city as alien territory. New York, it is said, is not one city but a collection of such neighborhoods whose ties to each other loosen by the year. Social workers in Chicago tell us that there are children living within the Loop who have never seen Lake Michigan, three or four blocks away. These are the children who grow up never really "seeing" the life world of people who live in Oak Park and Cicero, not to speak of Evanston. Doubtless there are Evanstonians who have never seen the slums of the Loop, either. Psychologically, neither the slum dwellers nor the suburbanites reside in a place so large as Chicago. They have no image of the city as a human whole.

Life in big cities, in short, assails us daily with the suspicion that "What it all means, no one can say." Variety, pluralism, *perpetual* collision of dreams become our regular expectation as American urbanites. In our cities, it is difficult to be sure that any story could ever include a cast of characters as diverse as the ones we meet every day on the city street.

Is there such a story? If in spite of everything you are not yet ready to answer a resolute "no," please accept our invitation to read on.

LOOKING IN THE PAST FOR THE FUTURE

Edmund Burke once said: "People will not look forward to posterity who never look backward to their ancestors." The truth in that could also be phrased: You will despair about the future if there was nothing in your ancestors that you deem worth preserving for your posterity. To have identified such ancestors, such a past, is to have a cause to serve, a story to tell whose end is not yet.

No modern scientist has expressed the Burkean truth more eloquently than Loren Eiseley in describing the uniqueness of "human nature." Physiologically Homo sapiens is remarkable for a brain that seems unique in nature for its capacity to inject change into the world through language, tools, and social organization.

> Through language, this creature could communicate his dreams around the cave fires. Inevitably, a great wealth of intellectual diversity, and consequent selective mating, based upon mutual attraction, would emerge from the dark storehouse of nature. The cruel and the gentle would sit at the same fireside, dreaming already in the Stone Age the different dreams they dream today.
>
> The visionary was already awaiting the eternal city; the gifted musician sat hearing in his brain sounds that did not yet exist. All waited upon and yet possessed, in some dim way, the future in their heads. Abysmal darkness and great light lay invisibly about their camps. The phantom cities of the far future awaited latent talents for which, in that unspecialized time, there was no name.
>
> Above all, some of them, a mere handful in any generation perhaps, loved—they loved the animals about them, the song of the wind, the soft voices of women. On the flat surfaces of the cave walls the three dimensions of the outside world took animal shape and form. Here—not with the ax, not with the bow—man fumbled at the door of his true kingdom. Here, hidden in times of trouble behind silent brows, against the man with the flint, waited St. Francis of the birds.[5]

These paragraphs from the mind of an honest modern man tell us something important about how we *let* the past influence our present. We make choices between the people of the past whom we are glad to acclaim as "our people" and the rest who may be our biological but not our culturally *cherished* ancestors. In this context, one's choice of ancestors is a shifty matter. About some of them we are likely to be notably silent. A citizen of the Commonwealth of Massachusetts rarely brags that her Pilgrim Fathers included a large number of indentured slaves, or a citizen of Georgia that his ancestors were brought to Savannah in chains. *The past we celebrate pre-enacts the future we hope for.* Not the Tories, but the Patriots, are the Americans who were celebrated in the Bicentennial. Yet if one were still hoping for a recolonization of the United States by the British, one might indeed celebrate the Tories. Either Genghis Khan or St. Francis could be your hero, but hardly both.

Consciously or unconsciously, most human beings down through the centuries have defined themselves in their sense of identification with certain of their ancestors. When most conscious of the story they are acting in, they start the story by telling about somebody who preceded them, often with attention to a future hope which, like all human futures, remains uncertain. This book is written in this double bind. On the one hand, we have hope for the lives of people like Harrisene Little and Philip Delaney, who live, at once together and alienated, in the cities of America. We share an intuition that in such persons the human race really is "fumbling at the door" of our "true kingdom" whose "phantom cities of the far future" have yet to be built. On the other hand, we write out of a complementary memory that undergirds and provokes this very hope. We identify from the start with a certain set of human beings in the past—the early Hebrews and Christians—whose historic, particular stories provide us clues to the plot of the great story of humanity itself. We are curious to understand the impact of those stories upon our own stories, especially the perplexing questions they raise about how we are to live, until we die, in the cities of America.

Chapter 2

Hebrew Hints
to City Dwellers

If scholars are right, the earth has been peopled for one million years. Traces of human cities go back a mere five thousand years. So the urban age of human history is young.

The major world religions are equally young. In the case of the Hebrew and Christian faiths, their stories can hardly be told without the mention of certain historic cities. In the first telling, those cities do not come off as nice places.

The early Hebrews, in fact, took a decidedly negative view of city life. Had you been present when that history was taking shape, you would have understood their deep-rooted suspicion of "the big city." Imagine, for example, listening to a nameless slave at the end of a weary day sometime in the thirteenth century B.C., in a city called Pithom, east of the Nile River.

"Why are we building this city? Because Pharaoh wants a place to store surplus grain to keep his loyal subjects well fed in time of drought, to make his armies strong enough to threaten his disloyal subjects, and to make more slaves of people like us and the Ethiopians. We build him storehouses and temples and monstrous tombs, and it all adds up to forging our own chains. These Egyptians and their cities—they keep the bricks and throw away the brickmakers. We're the chaff, and the bricks are their grain! Don't tell me about cities: they're all like old Babel from before Abraham's time. They're all built on the backs of poor people to make 'glory' for people like Pharaoh. What does the story say? 'Let us build ourselves a city and a tower with its top in the heavens, and make a name for ourselves; or we shall be dispersed all over the earth.' Well, the Lord had a way of dealing with that! He spread them over the earth; he put an end to the building of *that* city. I wish he'd put an end to the building of this one and send us to a land of our own.

"I say, back to Abraham! Give us the mountains again, or even the desert. He left the cities of the Two Rivers. I say let's leave the cities of the Nile! When I said that to my wife the other day, she looked troubled. 'How would we eat out there on the desert?' It was a hard question to answer, but I said: 'The same way Abraham ate. And one day we shall have the land promised him. And even if it took a long time to get such a land, better the desert than slavery. In Pithom we build our own prison; in the desert we would be free.'

"But my answer didn't satisfy her. She said: 'The *Lord* called Abraham. We could only do it if we knew that he called us too. There's Ramses, and Ra, and his armies: how could we oppose all that unless the Lord were on our side?' She's right, you know. My brother spent five years building one of those temples for their god Ra over in Memphis. He's convinced that Ra really does fight for the Egyptians. My wife will have to be right before my brother sets a foot on that desert. But now you know what my prayer is—in the cool of the morning, under the whip at high noon, and in my bone-weariness at night? *God of Abraham and Joseph, make us free!*"[1]

Given knowledge of the Bible, no one is likely to find such an interview altogether imaginary. The ancient Hebrews had good reason to hate cities. Their post-Egypt experience was to add more reason yet. Before we explore those additions, we may raise a question that almost any late-twentieth-century reader is bound to ask. Just because the ancient Hebrews believed that a divine power "brought them up out of Egypt," are we required to believe the same? City life was oppressive for them. Must we believe that their "Lord" had something to do with delivering them from that oppression?

We will not attempt a long answer to that question. But here is a short illustrative answer from the depths of recent twentieth-century history:

There are captivities in our own society that get broken only by the power of "a story about the whole world that gives the storyteller a time, a place, and a role in it"—that is, the power of a religious faith. Such a captivity, which in many ways was worse for the Jewish people than their captivity in Egypt, was their captivity to the Nazis during World War II. Called the Holocaust by contemporary Jewish students of the event, the Nazi project to exterminate Judaism came so close to achievement that many surviving Jews see in it evidence that the God of Abraham and Joseph is *not,* in fact, a power at work in the world liberating anybody from captivity. In the whole, horrible death-camp story, however, there were occasional testimonies to the power of the Jewish faith to move its adherents to pray—and to act —like their brickmaker-ancestors of old. Perhaps the most fearful testimony of all came from an annihilation camp near Treblinka, fifty miles from Warsaw. The Nazis planned here to kill a million Jews from Poland and the Balkan countries. As in other such camps, they used the prisoners themselves to "staff" their organization of death. (As frequently pointed out by historians, the death camps of the Nazis were the product of a match between a diabolical political philosophy and the "high" technology of an urbanized civilization. The camps presupposed railroads, automobiles, radio, firearms, nationally coordinated bureaucracy, and the selective use of the social and biological sciences. By comparison, the tyranny of the ancient Pharaohs was technically primitive.)

Casual recollectors of the Nazi nightmare have frequently wondered how the Jews themselves so regularly worked in the extermination of their own kind. Also: how did so many people go to their sure deaths without frequent mass attempts to revolt? One of the successful camp revolts provided an answer with gruesome eloquence, as readers of the novelized account, *Treblinka,* by Jean-François Steiner, will remember.[2] First, the Nazis were masters of the arts of deceptive hope. At every step on the way to the gas chambers, prisoners had hope dangled before their eyes—the hope of survival. Second, they managed to parcel out such hope person by person: making every prisoner's hope of survival depend upon his or her willingness to cooperate in the destruction of other prisoners. "The skill of the Germans was to *serialize* the Jews and to prevent these series from becoming groups."[3] On these two bits of psychology, the society of the death camps was efficiently organized. At Treblinka, some 800,000 persons had been destroyed before a tiny minority looked back at the history of the suffering of the Jewish people and said to one another: "We are a chapter in that history. But the Nazis mean to bury us all here so completely that none of us lives even to tell the story. If we do not care enough about the past and the future of the Jews to value our story more than our own lives, will anyone want to be a Jew anymore?" On the grounds of that shared *theology*, six hundred persons planned a revolt whose one overriding aim was: "Get at least one witness out to tell the story of Treblinka, to make it a part of the recorded history of the Jews." The bloody event yielded only forty persons who escaped to tell the tale; and of this number only six survived World War II.

Was the Treblinka revolt "worth it" to the Jewish people? The question is not far from kindred questions such as: "Was the march through the desert under Moses worth it? the captivity in Babylon? the destruction of Jerusalem by the Romans? the suffering of a thousand pogroms under supposedly Christian kings?" The only way to answer such questions is out of one's own religion, one's own account of what story, if any, is being told from generation to generation of the human race. The minimal lesson of the Treblinka revolt is the enormous organizing power of a life story that sweeps up the lives of individuals and generations, enabling them to confess together: "We are not the authors of this drama, but we are essential actors in it. We serve the Author, if need be, by our very deaths!"

THE GREAT DELIVERER OF THE CAPTIVES: BABYLON AND BEYOND

The Bible remains an opaque book for many of us moderns. *That* strenuous a faith, so historically comprehensive and so personally demanding, is hard for the television generation to appropriate. Doubtless if they had known that forty years of wandering lay before them in Sinai, some of those Hebrew brickmakers in Egypt would have shrunk from the effort. As it turned out, no one who left Egypt lived to see the milk and honey of another land. You had to live for a cause that outlasted your own generation even to embark on the trek out of Egypt.

Many affluent modern Americans are uncertain of any such cause. We are secular, in the original Latin sense of the word: we are prisoners of our own particular *saeculum*, or "age." Like Alex Haley, who went searching for his ancestors in Africa and recorded his search in his book *Roots,* we can only take a long look into our future if we can also take a deep look back into our past. "How can I see where I am going when I don't know where I came from?"[4]

Their historic roots, Moses and his successors believed, went back to the original Hebrew, Abraham, and to his life-style of *pilgrimage.* Human existence is a journey, leaving something behind, headed somewhere worth traveling to. In this faith, humans see themselves as "passing travellers on earth . . . looking for a country of their own" (Heb. 11:13–14).

What kind of country have such Hebrew-Christian "travellers" been looking for? Anyone interested in the question can turn to the Bible. A pertinent place to turn to is The Book of Jeremiah.

That prophet of the seventh to the sixth century B.C. is pertinent for any book treating the theme "No Continuing City," because no biography in the Old Testament is more appropriately summarized in that very phrase. His birthplace was the little town of Anathoth, not far from Jerusalem, the big city of his country. When he first started visiting it as a child, Jerusalem was four hundred years old. The memory of his people's deliverance from Egypt was some seven hundred years old. Like the prophets before him, Jeremiah looked out upon his own times through the lenses of all seven of those centuries. Without the spectacles of Exodus, Wilderness Wandering, Canaan Conquest and Occupation, he would have been blind to the presence of God in the local, national, and international daily news. Before they closed in death, the eyes of Jeremiah filtered a lot of such news. Behind it all he perceived the power who had brought his nation up out of Egypt. In virtually his first word to young Jeremiah, that God of power had said:

> . . . kings shall come and each shall set up his throne
> before the gates of Jerusalem,
> against her walls on every side,
> and against all the cities of Judah.
> I will state my case against my people
> for all the wrong they have done in forsaking me,
> in burning sacrifices to other gods,
> worshipping the work of their own hands.
> Brace yourself, Jeremiah.[5]
>
> (Jer. 1:15–17a)

What sad ironies that "word" must have set echoing in the halls of Jeremiah's historical memory! They had been delivered from the tyranny of Pharaoh and his idols only to fall into a new captivity to idols of their own choosing. Now on the horizon of history crouched the armies of a new tyrant whose capital city Babylon had for mythological ages symbolized to the Hebrews the perils of idolatry. The Lord was about to use Babylon the idolater to overthrow Jerusalem the idolater.

How had Judah lost touch with its origins? It had been from very early times, Jeremiah must have remembered. The Wilderness years and the two centuries of the Conquest had swirled around two large political-religious issues: *spiritual idolatry* and *social injustice.* In a day when it is easy to separate two such notions, we are likely to be puzzled that the Biblical prophets associated the two so closely. The "worship of false gods" sounds like a sin impossible to an age that would as soon dispense with gods altogether. Moral injustice, on the other hand, seems to hang around human societies ad infinitum.

Remembering Egypt, the Hebrews were more realistic. Their descendants were more realistic about Adolf Hitler too. In all ancient civilizations, especially rich and powerful ones like Egypt and Assyria, political power and religious worship had close, institutionalized connection. The battle between rival claimants to the throne in Egypt often took place in terms of rival gods whom the Pharaoh worshiped. The temples which the Pharaohs built were consolidations of their power. Doubtless Ramses believed that he was adding honor to the great god Ra by using slaves to build monuments to Ra—and to himself, the royal kinsman of his god. The link between religion and politics was blatant. The only way for a Moses to revolt against political oppression was to revolt against the religious order that underlay that oppression.

From Moses to Jeremiah the prophets were constantly alert to the connection between what people worshiped and how they behaved toward each other—between their "faith" and their "ethics." The "oldest profession" may be either prostitution *or* the cultic priesthood. The combination of both was common and profitable among the cults of the eastern Mediterranean. "Sex and sanctity for sale": an unbeatable pitch! More subtle was the worship of the gods of agricultural fertility or Baalism. If one were a farmer, was there anything wrong with spending money and time in a temple for the success of one's crops? Yes, said the prophets: to worship material success is to devote one's life to a gift of the Creator rather than to the Creator himself. Further, the worship of the material leads directly to the exploitation of one's neighbor on behalf of the material. From worship of Baal, to worship of wealth, to oppression of the poor: an effortless transition belonging to the seamless integrity of one corrupt life-style!

Any good thing, lifted to supreme, worshipful status, can become a corruption. This old truth of the Hebrew-Christian faith remains as basic to that faith as ever it was three thousand years ago. The goods of human life—knowledge, wealth, strength—are the great rivals of the Best, the Lord of all being. Jeremiah uttered his convictions on this score when he relayed "words of the Lord" like these:

> Let not the wise man boast of his wisdom
>   nor the valiant of his valour;
> let not the rich man boast of his riches;
>   but if any man would boast, let him boast of this,
>   that he understands and knows me.
> For I am the LORD, I show unfailing love,
>   I do justice and right upon the earth;
>   for on these I have set my heart.
>
> (Jer. 9:23–24)

Idol worship, the prophets constantly repeat, promises the idolater a limited good at the price of the unlimited good. Jeremiah's quarrel with his fellow citizens of Jerusalem circles back regularly to this point: You organize your personal lives and the life of this city around wealth, or power, or the delights of religious ceremony, when you could be organizing around the unfailing love and justice of the Lord. The result for you and your city will be the deterioration of your life from within and without. Your inward religious deceit overflows even now in social injustice, and all this sets the stage for your political defeat at the hands of an external enemy. Standing in the gateway of the Temple one day, Jeremiah put it this way:

> Listen to the words of the LORD. . . . You keep saying, "This place is the temple of the LORD, the temple of the LORD!" This catchword of yours

is a lie; put no trust in it. Mend your ways and your doings, deal fairly with one another, do not oppress the alien, the orphan, and the widow, shed no innocent blood in this place . . . in the land which I gave long ago to your forefathers for all time. You gain nothing by putting your trust in this lie. You steal, you murder, you commit adultery and perjury, you burn sacrifices to Baal, you run after other gods whom you have not known; then you come and stand before me in this house, which bears my name, and say, "We are safe"; safe, you think, to indulge in all these abominations. Do you think that this house, this house which bears my name, is a robbers' cave? (Jer. 7:2–11)

The words are plain enough, but the tune is hard for modern ears to catch. What does this have to do with the way modern human beings organize their lives, say, in the cities of America? The answer will be slow, but sure, we hope, in coming in the pages of this book. For the moment, notice the *untrivial, comprehensive, systematic* character of Jeremiah's moral analysis of his own society. What people treat as ultimate in their lives—what they worship—has an impact on one strand of their lives after another. Eventually things come down to the corruption of the total fabric. Jeremiah saw this clearly in the connection between idolatry and the assorted sins of public and private citizens in Jerusalem. A king who is "soft on Baalism" finds it natural to finance his palace by omitting to pay wages to his workers. This is the king whom Jeremiah describes as one who has "no thought for anything but gain" (Jer. 22:16–17). If one understands Baalism, can one be surprised at that conclusion? Again, having compromised the best truth that they knew in worship, many citizens found it easy to compromise the truth in personal and public affairs. "Lying, not truth, is master in the land," laments Jeremiah; and over his own, the prophet's ear can hear the divine lament, "For me they care nothing." (Jer. 9:3.) The result is that they come to care nothing for one another, either:

> Be on your guard, each man against his friend;
>   put no trust even in a brother.
> Brother supplants brother,
> and a friend slanders friend.
> They make game of their friends
>   but never speak the truth.

(Jer. 9:4–5)

Nobody trusts anyone anymore, because a truly dependable, trust-worthy object of loyalty is missing from personal, interpersonal, and social existence. As a twentieth-century poet put it, "things fall apart," because "the center cannot hold."[6] Or, as a modern sociologist might put it: you can observe, through the eyes of Jeremiah, the cost that any society pays for the decay of its consensus about the central meaning of membership in that society. The rush to idol worship in ancient Judah and modern America is really very human: human persons and groups seem easily captivated by one fad after another. But faddism disperses loyalties; it substitutes alleged needs of the moment for long-term commitments between neighbors. "They run from one sin to another," cried Jeremiah (Jer. 9:3), a pattern easily discerned in their running from one place of worship to another:

> You, Judah, have as many gods as you have towns; you have set up as many altars to burn sacrifices to Baal as there are streets in Jerusalem. (Jer. 11:13)

That is the heart of Jeremiah's indictment of idolatry as moral, not merely ceremonial, corruption. Human sin is "born in the doubt, nourished by anxiety, which leads to a self-assertion that does not wait on God."[7] The end of idolatry is akin to its beginning: the proud, anxious preoccupation of humans with their own needs of the moment. Idolatry is the great secularizer; it narrows, and narrows, and narrows human concern to the immediate; it cuts persons and societies off from the broad horizon; it turns the human commitment away from great causes to things petty, trivial, and immediate.

We can now appreciate why Jeremiah and other Old Testament prophets voiced a deep-flowing skepticism about the moral-religious quality of *cities*. Amos knew that idolatry and economic exploitation could flourish in the countryside too. Rural living is no guarantee of innocence. But the farmers of Israel, in the eighth century B.C., sold much of their produce in the city of Bethel. There the greed of middlemen fed on the commercial innocence of the farmers with reinforcement from priests and government officials who winked at profit-gouging to their own profit. By their *systematic* conniving, cried Amos,

> They grind the heads of the poor into the earth
> and thrust the humble out of their way.
>
> (Amos 2:7a)

No wonder "city life" fell under the suspicious gaze of the prophets. "You, Judah, have as many gods as you have towns!" (Jer. 2:28.) The earliest kings—Saul and David—encountered that suspicion in the prophet Samuel. He predicted that the coming of kings of Israel would bring idolatry, tyranny, and exploitation. The history of kings in Jerusalem abundantly confirmed the prophecy. (Cf. I Sam. 8: 11–18.)

Is it possible to build a city in which the true God is worshiped truly and citizens deal with one another, every day of their lives, justly and mercifully? Is it possible that a city might rise on some hill, worthy of the reputation of a *city of God?* For a thousand years that question was to haunt the theology, the politics, the public and the private reflection of people high and low in the city of Jerusalem. It haunted Jeremiah, who lived to see Jerusalem fall. The Babylonians finally conquered it, dragging its most able citizens off to Babylon in chains, dispersing the rest of the population, ravishing Solomon's Temple, toppling the walls begun by David. Jeremiah's grim vision was fulfilled:

> . . . Jerusalem a heap of ruins, a haunt of wolves,
> and the cities of Judah an unpeopled waste.
>
> (Jer. 9:11. Cf. Micah 3:12)

HOPE FOR CITY DWELLERS?

Before his death, Jeremiah was granted a peek into a different future. Hardly had the last chariot rumbled through the suburban village of his birth before the great doomsayer was visited by another vision:

> The time is coming, says the LORD, when the city shall be rebuilt in the LORD's honor from the Tower of Hananel to the Corner Gate. (Jer. 31:38)

> The time will come when houses, fields, and vineyards will again be bought and sold in this land. (Jer. 32:15)

I hid my face from this city because of their wicked ways, but now I will bring her healing; I will heal and cure Judah and Israel, and will let my people see an age of peace and security. (Jer. 33:5–6)

You say of this place, "It is in ruins, and neither man nor beast lives in the cities of Judah or in the streets of Jerusalem. It is all a waste, inhabited by neither man nor beast." Yet in this place shall be heard once again the sounds of joy and gladness, the voice of the bridegroom and the bride; here too shall be heard voices shouting, "Praise the LORD of Hosts, for he is good, for his love endures for ever," as they offer praise and thanksgiving in the house of the LORD. For I will restore the fortunes of the land as once they were. This is the word of the LORD. (Jer. 33:10–11)

Just as the destruction of a great city was the climax of divine judgment, so the restoration of that city would be the climax of divine blessing. All the elements of the old corrupt city would be there in the new city—religion, politics, commerce, wealth, marriage. But the mixture, the systematic relationships, would be different. They would be organized around a center of praise of One who is good and loving forever. And out of such worship would grow justice, loyalty, and mercy in the whole cloth of human affairs. Such, at least, was the hope of the prophet.[8]

The newly deported Jerusalemites took this vision with them to Babylon. Its towers had long symbolized to them the religious pride and imperial oppression of "a land of idols that glories in its dreaded gods" (Jer. 50:38). But with superb theological consistency, Jeremiah sweeps up Babylon, too, into the whirlwind of divine judgment that was already howling through Jerusalem.

O opulent city, standing beside great waters,
your end has come, your destiny is certain.
(Jer. 51:13)

Though Babylon should reach to the skies
and make her high towers inaccessible,
I will send marauders to overrun her.
. . . .
The walls of broad Babylon shall be razed to the
ground,
her lofty gates shall be set on fire.

> Worthless now is the thing for which the nations toiled;
> the peoples wore themselves out for a mere nothing.
> (Jer. 51:53, 58)

One scholar has said of the prophets, all that is strong falls under the lash of their denunciation.[9] And all that is weak seems to command their special compassion. We live in a world, said Walter Rauschenbusch, in which "the strong have quite enough power to protect their own interests, and power left over to protect their unjust interests as well." Jeremiah envisions a city—a nation, a world community—which reflects the very character of God: power in the service of justice and love. It was an exalted vision: a human community in which "religion" is so real that the institutions of religion fade away:

> I will set my law within them and write it on their hearts; I will become their God and they shall become my people. No longer need they teach one another to know the LORD; all of them, high and low alike, shall know me. (Jer. 31:33–34)

Would such a "religiously real" society have any peculiar geographical relationship to a historic place called Jerusalem? It is startling to realize how long ago the question was planted in the Hebrew mind. *Disagreement* over the answer is as much a factor in the geopolitical world of A.D. 1977 as news about the State of Israel is a factor in every daily newspaper. In an intriguing way, Jeremiah posed for Christians and Jews, ancient and modern, almost all the basic questions of religious faith as it relates to the history of *this* particular city. Does the meaning of history center upon the meaning of Jerusalem? Three major religious faiths in the modern world answer some form of "yes" to that question. Is historic Jerusalem a peculiar location of evil in human affairs? a peculiar location of good? To whom does Jerusalem "belong"—Jews, Christians, Moslems, the world? What does Jerusalem, ancient or modern, have to teach the world?

In that turning point of Hebrew history called the Babylonian exile, with the prophecies of Jeremiah stuck forever in their memories, the Jerusalem captives began their great debate on these questions. If the prophet had been right about the divine judgment upon Jerusalem, he must be right about the divine restoration as well. To Jerusalem the captives must someday return! Yes, indeed, writes aging Jeremiah from devastated Judah. But in the meantime, there is a spiritual discipline that you must learn. Learn how to "sing the LORD's song in a foreign land" (Ps. 137:4). Be in no hurry to return to ruined Jerusalem. Settle down. Don't assume that God is any less present to you in Babylon than he was in Jerusalem.

> Build houses and live in them; plant gardens and eat their produce. Marry wives and beget sons and daughters; take wives for your sons and give your daughters to husbands, so that they may bear sons and daughters and you may increase there and not dwindle away. Seek the welfare of any city to which I have carried you off, and pray to the LORD for it; on its welfare your welfare will depend. (Jer. 29:5–7)

The exiles in Babylon obeyed this advice from Jeremiah. They obeyed it so well that when opportunities came for their posterity to return to Jerusalem, some stayed on in Babylon. They established a community of exiles, the first great expression of the Dispersion, and eventually they became one of the great centers of Jewish life and culture. Indeed, in the years just after their forced departure from "the courts of the LORD," they invented a new institution for the perpetuation of the Hebrew life story. The *synagogue* became the place where the exiles could gather to study the law of Moses, to hear the prophetic "words," and to encourage one another in the life practices that set Jews apart from Babylonians. Here in the synagogue, the *meaning* of Jerusalem could be celebrated, perpetuated, handed on to a new generation. Jerusalem had its own citizens practicing their citizenship in the heart of Babylon! [10]

It was a development heavy with promise for the future of the Jewish people in world history. It was equally heavy for the origin of a people to be called Christian. To that origin, and its significance for the welfare and the troubles of human cities, the next chapter attends.

Chapter 3

"In Jerusalem . . . and to the Ends of the Earth"

To call oneself a "Christian" surely means to focus one's life upon a man named Jesus.

In this chapter we want to examine some impacts this man made upon people who first encountered him in his own time. A few words linking that time to Jeremiah's are in order.

Back from Babylon, a remnant of the Hebrew people did rebuild Jerusalem. But their descendants' lot for the next five centuries was to be continued captivity to oppressive world empires. A Babylonian empire fell to a Persian, a Persian to a Greek, and a Greek to a Roman —the longest-enduring empire of the ancient Mediterranean world. Hebrew history and Hebrew faith, during all five of these centuries, interlocked with the politics of imperialism, as during ten previous centuries. So, whatever else it meant to call oneself a Jew, it surely meant identification with a people who had *survived* the political oppression of all these centuries. They had *practiced* their religion in their own communities spread around the Mediterranean basin. They had practiced it most fully in the city of *Jerusalem*. The heart of their identity as a people still focused on that city. Their hope for its liberation from the power of Roman legions repeated the hopes of all their ancestors. They had seen the Lord of history most clearly at work when he was freeing his people from the Egyptians, the Philistines, the Assyrians, the Babylonians, the Persians, and the Greeks.

Unsympathetic contemporaries must have accused the Jews of being obsessed with their own political independence. The Romans, among others, considered themselves enlightened rulers. Among all their conquered provinces, Judaea alone had a local religion whose leaders seemed obstinately incapable of enjoying the law and order which Rome brought to the nations under its control. In their Jerusalem Temple, the Jews had a courtyard into which no non-Jew could set foot on pain of death. These descendants of Moses still defined themselves according to the ancient confession: "So we shall be distinct, I and thy people, from all the peoples on earth." (Ex. 33:16.) Gentiles interpreted this stance of the Jew as contempt for the rest of the world and, humanly enough, returned the contempt. The relations of Jews and Romans, in the years we now call the first century, were brittle and smoldering. Jesus was born only decades before an explosion that would shatter the attachment of the Jewish community to its ancient Promised Land as it had never been shattered even by the Babylonians.

So, when he visited the Holy City for the first time at the age of twelve, Jesus of Nazareth was among the last of his people to worship on the great Temple site chosen by David and Solomon. Sixty years later, in an act of exasperated imperial violence, the Romans would level the place to the ground. Then for nineteen hundred years, it could be said of the Jewish people that they literally had "no continuing city" (Heb. 13:14).

"THE KINGDOM OF GOD IS UPON YOU"

From even so brief a sketch of his time and place, we can gather some notion of the fear, hope, curiosity, and confusion that stirred in the minds of the people who first heard the thirty-year-old Jesus make a public speech. It began with the words:

The time has come; the kingdom of God is upon you; repent, and believe the Gospel. (Mark 1:14-15)

For the next three years his audiences would ask him, ask each other, and ask diverse authorities what the man meant by "the kingdom of God." The question for them resonated with the tortured history of kings and kingdoms here in this little country over a millennium. Many centuries later, we still wonder what he meant by the Kingdom of God; but the crisp New Testament record leaves no doubt that he considered himself as *bringer* of this Kingdom. A new political order is brewing, and he is its catalyst. But like the leaven to which he compared the Kingdom itself, he brings this new order quietly and with casual ordinariness:

> Jesus was walking by the Sea of Galilee when he saw Simon and his brother Andrew on the lake at work with a casting-net; for they were fishermen. Jesus said to them, "Come with me, and I will make you fishers of men." And at once they left their nets and followed him. (Mark 1:16–17)

As one reads these verses from the first page of the earliest summary of the story—the Gospel of Mark—it is easy to forget to be astonished. Most of us grew up hearing the names Jesus, Simon Peter, and Andrew as household words. And even if we are rather dubious about many things associated with the Christian religion, we are historically knowledgeable enough to know that Jeremiah and Jesus and Simon Peter are among the most celebrated figures in Western and even world history. Easily missed in this common knowledge, however, is the *perception* required for anyone in the first century A.D. to think of putting people like Jesus, not to speak of Simon and Andrew, into a history book. In that thought lies the beginning of a great revolution. In a profound sense, the revolution is political.

A modern scholar who saw the revolution clearly was Erich Auerbach.[1] Unique among the literature of its time, says Auerbach, the New Testament begins with incidents like the one we have just recalled: a carpenter from a country town engaging in important conversation with "unimportant" fishermen. He has just announced the coming of the Kingdom of God, and he immediately invites two day laborers to participate in the event! No Greek or Roman writer would have begun to record any "historic" occasion so, says Auerbach. The Roman historian Tacitus, for example, chronicles the world conquests of Rome's legions without ever portraying Roman soldiers as serious persons. Soldiers, for Tacitus, are part of a class of ordinary people who have their useful place in society but who, if they enter the history books as individuals, do so as objects of humor and ridicule. Really serious persons for Tacitus tend to be senators and generals, just as the heroes and heroines of Greek tragedy tend to be aristocrats. Why should anyone want to write history beginning with a carpenter and two fishermen?[2]

The New Testament answer to that question is boldly theological: God wants to write history that way. Just as he revealed the meaning of history in his liberation of obscure slaves from Egypt, so he continues now to "establish righteousness on the earth" by lifting obscure, humble people into the status of heroes and heroines of a world drama. The opening chapters of all the Gospel narratives say as much, and the opening chapters of Luke are especially eloquent on the point. Here the mother of Jesus "tells out the greatness of the Lord" because she believes that "humble as she is" a great event is about to happen through her.

> The arrogant of heart and mind he has put to rout,
> he has brought down monarchs from their thrones,
>   but the humble have been lifted high.
> The hungry he has satisfied with good things,
>   the rich sent empty away.
>
> He has ranged himself at the side of Israel his servant;
>   firm in his promise to our forefathers,
> he has not forgotten to show mercy to Abraham
>   and his children's children, for ever.
>
>   (Luke 1:51–55)

Those of us who read such words nineteen hundred years later can only experience their "good news" quality if we know what it is like:

> to think of oneself as a nobody;
> to be reminded every day that one is powerless to say "no" to
>   some circumstance of one's life;
> to expect *other* people to do the important things;
> to expect that one's own death will not matter much to anybody.

Perhaps every one of us has some of these feelings; but little or much, the Gospel narratives impress the reader with this fact: *Jesus of Nazareth made nobodies feel like somebodies.* The story tells us dozens of ways in which it happened: he listens to the groans of the sick. He looks for food for the hungry. He stops by the road to talk with children, women, and beggars. He gathers a miscellany of disciples around him, almost all of them poor peasants from Galilee; calls them "the light of the world"; encourages them to call the Great God

of the Universe by an intimate domestic name; and otherwise con-
vinces them that "the kingdom of God is upon you" with an im-
mediacy that makes "you" a participant in an event on the center
stage of history.

The message had powerful results in the lives of people in the
Gospel narratives. Midway in the story (Matt. 16:13–28), Jesus gives
a former fisherman a new name—Peter—as the foundation rock of
a new human structure to be called "my church." But the mystery
of this new status for an ordinary Galilean peasant is overshadowed
at once by another mystery:

> From that time Jesus began to make it clear to his disciples that he had
> to go to Jerusalem, and there to suffer much from the elders, chief priests,
> and doctors of the law; to be put to death and to be raised again on the
> third day. (Matt. 16:21)

Latter-day Christians have always found Simon Peter a peculiarly
convincing historic witness to the meaning of faith in Jesus as bringer
of the Kingdom of God. In the further events of Peter's life they see
someone who "cared for his own safety," as human beings dearly love
to do; and someone who was taught by Jesus to "lose himself" for the
sake of Jesus and those other people whom Jesus called "the least of
these my brethren." The best-known part of his story is Peter's denial
of any association with Jesus during the final hours of the trial and
crucifixion in Jerusalem. So vivid are all four of the Gospel narratives
here that we have no trouble understanding the human reality of this
event. We recognize our own vulnerability to the human weakness
displayed by Peter, and share the terrible mixture of fear and shame
that must have ensued in him. As Auerbach so eloquently describes
this incident:

> Peter . . . was a fisherman from Galilee of humblest background and
> humblest education. The other participants in the night scene in the
> court of the High Priest's palace are servant girls and soldiers. From the
> humdrum existence of his daily life, Peter is called to the most tremen-
> dous role. Here, like everything else to do with Jesus' arrest, his appear-
> ance on the stage—viewed in the world-historical continuity of the
> Roman Empire—is nothing but a provincial incident, an insignificant
> local occurrence, noted by none but those directly involved. . . . Viewed

superficially, the thing is a police action and its consequences; it takes place entirely among everyday men and women of the common people; anything of the sort could be thought of in antique [classical Greek–Roman] terms only as farce or comedy. Yet why is it neither of these? Why does it arouse in us the most serious and most significant sympathy? Because it portrays something which neither the poets nor the historians of antiquity set out to portray: the birth of a spiritual movement in the depths of the common people, from within the everyday occurrences of contemporary life. . . . What we witness is the awakening of "a new heart and a new spirit." . . . What we see here is a world which on the one hand is entirely real, average, identifiable as to place, time, and circumstance, but which on the other hand is shaken in its very foundations, is transforming and renewing itself before our eyes.[3]

But the rest of Peter's story in the New Testament suggests that *we* would never have known about his failures if he had not gone on to experience a kind of success for which he gave Jesus absolute credit. Doubtless the details of Peter's denial were supplied by him to the early church. By the time he told the story, he had reversed some of the behavior recorded in it. Having once cringed before the political authorities (Matt. 26:56), he now had endured prison "for Jesus' sake" (Acts 12:1–5). Having once trembled to confess his friendship with Jesus to a certain maidservant (Matt. 26:69–75), he had now "preached Jesus and the resurrection" to thousands of people in Jerusalem and to the very authorities who had put Jesus to death (Acts 5:27–32). Having "wept bitterly" over his onetime cowardice, he was now living testimony to the presence of "the Spirit that raised Jesus from the dead." Had not that Spirit raised Peter, too, from a kind of death?

A single person, from death to life: that is one way to tell the story of the origin of the church of Jesus Christ in history. But there is some artificiality in such a telling, unless it is supplemented by another way.

ANOTHER WAY TO TELL IT

Peter's own experience bulged with the equally good news that Jesus is Lord of *the world.* What could that mean?

From a twentieth-century perspective, the "world" of two thousand years ago had to be a limited world indeed. The great majority of human beings, during all our million years on this planet, have lived in a world that extended only a few miles away from a campfire. Many modern people still live in such a world: some downtown Chicagoans, to remember one example. The centuries just prior to the birth of Jesus were remarkable, however, for the relative expansion of the perimeters of the "known world" in the minds of large numbers of people around the Mediterranean basin. Especially after the imperial exploits of Alexander the Great, many an educated Greek came to speak of "the whole inhabited earth," and they had a word for that: *oikoumenē*. From it, we get our word "ecumenical." The very concept was something of a revolution, parallel to our twentieth-century sense that we live in a global society.

In short, Jesus of Nazareth grew up in a world that was more nearly one political world than any that had ever been experienced by people a thousand miles around. Tyrannical as they were, the Roman emperors saw themselves as the coordinators and unifiers of a vast variety of tribes and nations bound together by the enlightenment of *lex Romana*. It was an *ecumenical* political order: a breathtaking achievement for many converts to it. What many contemporary Americans feel about the United States Constitution, innumerable participants in the Roman Empire felt about its ability to bring a tolerable peace between otherwise warring nations.

Any visitor to first-century Judaea would have detected there one of the great exceptions to this feeling about Rome. Neither in their culture nor in their practices did the descendants of Jeremiah rejoice in the new Roman universalism. They were resolute particularists. Had not the God of Moses chosen Israel for his special purposes in human history? How could Israel be faithful to its Lord while swearing to Rome the fidelity which its rulers demanded? To be sure, only in certain areas of organized society did Rome require its constituents to grant Rome absolute power: international relations, the army, certain tax policies, and certain areas of the legal system such as the administration of the death penalty for high crime. In other areas of life Rome's policy toward its captive territories was a live-and-let-live policy which in another time would be called liberal. But the shrewd military dictators who designed the *pax Romana* knew that at one point or another a social order cannot be liberal or subject merely to voluntary citizen compliance. Something unquestionable, a pragmatic absolute or dogma, lies at the foundation of every society. The Roman emperors were determined that in those key areas they would be the unquestionable rulers and protectors of the "common good."[4] To symbolize all this, they finally declared themselves gods, claiming for themselves (in eyes tutored by an Old Testament faith) that "specious ultimacy" which politicians, bereft of any other theory of authority, often claim for themselves. As Paul L. Lehmann suggests, societies have to solve the question of "sovereignty." They must find an "authentic point of order . . . the point around which the basic patterns of thought and life are organized and sustained and at which the issue between meaningful unity and meaningless disunity is resolved."[5]

Jesus was born "under" Augustus Caesar, the emperor who had first declared himself divine. Everywhere in the Empire, virtually in every town square, the Roman government had installed statues of the emperor which functioned as the imperial flag. Once a year, in a display of loyalty to the Empire, every citizen-subject was under legal order to gather in that town square and to salute the flag—to burn a bit of incense on the altar before the bust of the emperor. Doubtless people all over the Empire did their share of grumbling over this ceremony. But large numbers of them understood it merely as a gesture of respect for Rome in those areas of society where it demanded the right to rule. Other areas, including local religion, had their own legal place; the Romans wanted it so. Many surely must have conceded that the emperor was divine in only a limited sense. "You can pray to any god you want, and think what you want about that god's superiority to the emperor. All he wants is for you to accept his right to supremacy in practical politics. Your private religious beliefs are your own business."

At this point the descendants of Moses and Jeremiah drew a line, and otherwise shouted "no" in ways that left Roman, Greek, and barbarian alike dumbfounded. The easygoing accommodation of emperor worship and local religion seemed so practical, so statesmanlike, so politically wise. What kind of people would lay down their lives to prevent the bust of Caesar from being set up in the town square of Nazareth and (especially!) in the Jerusalem Temple? Answer: the self-confessed people of *The* Lord Almighty, Maker and Ruler of Heaven and Earth, beside whom all other claimants to authority are idols. For them the *first* question of human life is whether a person or a people worships this Lord who once overcame the idols of the Egyptian and who will as easily overcome the idols of the Roman.

"Why," the perplexed Roman must have retorted in exasperation, "*why* must the little matter of idol worship be so furiously resisted? Worship whom you want, just leave politics to us." But that was the sticking point at the heart of the Jewish faith: "We worship one who has so shaped our own community's life—what you call its 'politics' —that to abandon all these areas to you would be to abandon *Him*. Our nation began through the interference of our Lord in the politics of Egypt; we have no way to worship him as any other kind of authority. In *no* segment of this world does *he* abandon his authority to *you*. We will die before we pretend otherwise!"

Such an attitude earned for the Jews some grudging special concessions. The Romans decided to adjust. They permitted the Jews to dispense with the bust of the emperor in the towns and cities of Judaea. They exercised all the other political rights required of all the other provinces; but in Judaea no pinch of incense was likely to be smelled in public on the high Roman holiday.

Jesus of Nazareth and all who early chose to call themselves his disciples were imbued with the Jewish side of this argument. Though on at least two occasions Jesus suggested that paying taxes to Rome could be tolerated, the possibility of yielding to the Roman view on emperor worship he never suggests for a moment. To the contrary, in his one public confrontation with the local Roman government, he displays an unintimidated composure strongly reminiscent of Moses, Amos, Jeremiah, and all the other prophets who seemed little inclined to bow before kings and emperors. In one of the versions of the story, Pilate, the local Roman deputy, inquires of Jesus:

"Where have you come from? . . . Surely you know that I have authority to crucify you?" . . . "You would have no authority at all over me," Jesus replied, "if it had not been granted you from above." (John 19:8–11)

Whatever Pilate may have understood of this answer, he surely knew that for this Galilean teacher "above" did not mean "Rome." The issue of the trial before Pilate was Jesus' own claim to authority: Did he or did he not claim to be "King of the Jews"? Here in Pilate's own courtroom Jesus leads his human judge through some un-Roman, mostly Jewish theology lessons, the gist of which is: "My kingly authority comes from elsewhere" (John 18:37). Who grants an authority to Jesus that enables him to stand unintimidated before the representative of Rome? No one in that particular crowd was ready to say. But a few weeks later, a handful of people would begin to answer: "The God of Moses, the God of the prophets, he is the one: who now declares himself also the God and Father of our Lord Jesus!"

In that confession the possibility of a continuing discipleship to the man Jesus was born. That possibility, says the New Testament, became real in the resurrection of Jesus from the death that a political and a religious establishment had imposed on him. Now a former fisherman, who had recently shrunk from acknowledging his friendship with the Nazarene, cuts a very different public figure. Now he is a preacher of good news. To that still-hostile public he cries:

> The God of Abraham, Isaac, and Jacob, the God of our fathers, has given the highest honour to his servant, Jesus, whom you committed for trial and repudiated in Pilate's court—repudiated the one who was holy and righteous when Pilate had decided to release him. You begged as a favour the release of a murderer, and killed him who has led the way to life. But God raised him from the dead; of that we are witnesses. (Acts 3:13–15)

Did the resurrection of Jesus in fact initiate this preaching? The authority of Peter and his fellow witnesses alone has never been enough to compel others to answer "yes." Christian theologians (beginning with Paul) have often testified that belief in the resurrection of Jesus as an individual has less to do with the Christian life than the power of that life corporately through "the Spirit of him who raised Jesus." But one striking empirical event does compel attention: the rapid development of a new, living community of Christians soon after the crucifixion of Jesus. How was it humanly possible for a living church to rise so quickly? The minimal answer seems to be: the earliest "witnesses to the resurrection" had a convincing experience which made them convincing witnesses to the claim, "Jesus is Lord."

The corollary of that confession was both plain and dangerous:

The Roman emperor is *not* Lord. By asserting that corollary so loudly, these Jerusalem Christians, in effect, were being very good Jews. The stubborn Jewish resistance to public acknowledgment of the ultimate power of Rome in political affairs never received so powerful assistance as when the followers of Jesus began to claim that the God of Israel had raised him from the dead. For years the Christians in Jerusalem considered themselves faithful Jews, disagreeing with their fellows chiefly on the question of what place in his purpose the God of Israel had for Jesus of Nazareth. A second characteristic of this new Christian community, however, began to mark it as something larger than a subsection of the Jewish community: these people were missionaries far beyond the orb of the Jewish law. They had good news to tell, and they began to tell it to anyone who would listen. Not only did the authority of Jesus deliver them *from* the "powers" of the world; it freed them *for* the world. In the full Greco-Roman sense, that world was the *oikoumenē*.

How did the early Christians move from seeing themselves as a local Jewish sect to seeing themselves as an "ecumenical" network of Jesus' disciples? An illustration from the life of Simon Peter is probably the most vivid answer. The book of Acts pictures Peter as a man reborn in the resurrection of his friend Jesus, and empowered to be a new person in the coming of the "Spirit of him who raised Jesus." But access to the Spirit of God enables no human being to claim perfection, to make infallible judgments, or otherwise pretend that he or she has nothing more to learn. Of Jesus himself it is said that he learned obedience through what he suffered (Heb. 5:8). Of Peter and every other faithful disciple of Jesus the same had to be said.

Acts, chs. 10 and 11, records the most potent learning of Peter's career. For years he had preached the good news of Jesus—but only to fellow Jews. He had said that for over a thousand years the God of Israel had been preparing his people to live by his word and will. Who could understand Jesus or benefit from the power of his resurrection without deep, deep roots in the life of Israel? But the Spirit, who had overruled the high Roman governor and the high priest, was overruler of his church and its leaders too. Quite on his own, the Spirit prepares a Roman soldier named Cornelius to receive the good news of Jesus from the mouth of Peter. The events of Acts, chs. 10

and 11, ensue. Bewildered, knowing only that the Spirit commands him to do it, Peter walks for the first time in his life into the home of a Gentile. He talks about Jesus for the first time in his life to a Gentile family. Scarcely has he begun the talk "when the Holy Spirit came upon all who were listening to the message" (Acts 10:44). The meaning of the event dawns on Peter:

> I need not tell you that a Jew is forbidden by his religion to visit or associate with a man of another race; yet God has shown me clearly that I must not call any man profane or unclean. . . . I now see how true it is that God has no favourites, but that in every nation the man who is godfearing and does what is right is acceptable to him. (Acts 10:28, 34–35)

In the decade or so that followed the death of Jesus, nothing shaped the beginnings of the Christian movement so fundamentally as this event. Hushed and joyfully, the Christians in Jerusalem hear the news about Cornelius and come quickly to the conclusion: "This means that God has granted life-giving repentance to the Gentiles also." (Acts 11:18.) In one act of the Spirit in human affairs, the door of the Kingdom of God has been thrown open to the whole inhabited earth.

We can only understand the meaning of Peter's visit to Cornelius if we understand its link with both Judaism and the Roman Empire. The Christian community of the first century A.D. had roots in the one and fruits in the other. For its historical development, the Christian church is unimaginable apart from *both* Jerusalem and Rome.

During the five centuries since the Babylonian captivity, Judaism had discovered its own version of the *oikoumenē:* a network of synagogues spread about the Mediterranean, formed on the precedent of the Babylonian synagogue. Jerusalem was still the special city, and visits to its Temple by Jews from many countries still marked the annual festival of Passover. The very first group to proclaim themselves publicly as followers of the risen Jesus had been such an international mixture: "There were living in Jerusalem devout Jews drawn from every nation under heaven." (Acts 2:5.) Already this culturally diverse people, bound together by their practice of the Mosaic law, constituted a sociopolitical oddity in the ancient world. They belonged to no particular territory; they professed no conventional allegiance to the Roman emperor; and, if asked what "family" they belonged to, they answered "the people of God." Alone among the peoples of the first century B.C., they defined themselves neither as members of a particular political state nor by a particular family name. They were a sociological *tertium quid:* a third something standing apart from the private order of the family and the public order of politics. On such a split, Rome was seeking to build the unity of its empire. *But the Jewish example suggested another possibility: a human community drawn together around a single loyalty, not an infinitely split-up one.*

The formation of the Christian church represents an expansion and embodiment of this very possibility on a scale not envisioned by the leaders of Judaism then—or now. Marked off, with great early pain, from their parents-in-the-Lord, the early Christians found themselves burdened with a meaning and a task that were fruits of their own roots in the history of Israel. God's presence to the people of Israel was real and continuing, but the Spirit who raised Jesus from the dead had a larger presence in the world than could be symbolized by the Jerusalem Temple. His "people" had a membership of no limits. The community of Jews and the community of cultured Greeks both looked provincial now. Missionary preachers had discovered "barbarians" called in the name of Jesus to join the People of God! The idea of a universal religious fellowship had been born. A man named Jesus had come and

> proclaimed the good news: peace to you who were far off, and peace to those who were near by; for through him we both alike have access to the Father in the one Spirit. Thus you are no longer aliens in a foreign land, but fellow-citizens with God's people, members of God's household. You are built upon the foundation laid by the apostles and prophets, and Christ Jesus himself is the foundation-stone. In him the whole building is bonded together and grows into a holy temple in the Lord. In him you too are being built with all the rest into a spiritual dwelling. (Eph. 2:17–22)

A society whose ultimate judge and ruler was independent of every other human social authority, and a society to which every human being had an invitation: in these two radical principles the early Christian community found its bedrock foundations. In its historical context such a community was revolutionary. It still is.

THE REVOLUTIONARY CHRISTIAN COMMUNITY

To associate "revolution" with the Christian faith risks laughter from many a modern reader. How absurd to think of the First Presbyterian Church as revolutionary! We have paid diligent attention to the Old and New Testaments, however, to demonstrate that the First Presbyterian Church is heir to a revolutionary tradition. In their respective historical situations, both the ancient Jewish and the ancient Christian communities *were* revolutionary. They turned the wheel of human culture. They reset the cultural compass in radical ways.

We must focus for a while longer on those bands of Christians who lived in well-known cities of the Roman Empire. Many of the books of the New Testament bear their names: Ephesus, Philippi, Thessalonica, Corinth, Colossae, and Rome. Paul's letters to Christians in these cities signify a dispersion of the People of God which continues to this day. The practical results of over a millennium of the Biblical history get summarized in those early Christian communities. They provide our earliest clue to what "life in Christ," life in partnership with the Holy Spirit, looked like in its visible, human, *social* form. The new life was social in two respects: (1) one always sees individual Christians portrayed in their relationships with other Christians, usually in a local congregation; and (2) one always sees individual congregations making some impact on the larger environment of their society. These two dimensions are always intersecting in the New Testament picture of the young Christian church. In general, what picture do we see?

They worshiped God. They worshiped, believing that in Jesus the God of Isreal had granted all people a direct access to his personal presence. Above everything else, the early Christian communities were communities of prayer and praise. Remembering that Jesus rose from the dead on the first day of the week, they set aside Sunday as the day of worship. They thus began to reorganize their life world as humans in terms of *time.* To neglect to worship the Lord on "the Lord's day" would be to forget the most important event in all time. For the same reason, their commitment to corporate worship moved them toward a certain reorganization of *space* as well. First in their homes, occasionally in the open countryside, at times of persecution in caves and catacombs, and eventually in their own public buildings, they devoted social space to worship. Not asking the Romans for permission, they thus committed their first basic "crime against the state."

The accusation was not exactly absurd, as members of Germany's Confessing Church came to understand during the Nazi era. Theology, it turns out, can make a political difference in the world, as the enemies of Christ have sometimes realized more shrewdly than the Christians. One surviving evidence of this is a bit of correspondence between the Roman emperor Trajan and Pliny, his governor-designate in Bithynia in A.D. 111. Beware of *any* organization of people without a government "license," the emperor warns Pliny. Don't even trust firemen!

> You think that a society *(collegium)* of firemen might be formed at Nicomedia, as at many other places. But we must remember that your province has been especially disturbed by the factions arising from such institutions. Whatever name they bear, it is almost certain that men so united will become a political club. It will be better therefore to supply the necessary apparatus in case of fire, to warn the landlords to take precautions for themselves, and, in case of necessity, to make use of the populace in extinguishing fires.[6]

As T. R. Glover comments, Roman politicians were trying to avoid, like a plague, the rise of any hope among their subjects "that there was an alternative to the Roman empire and the existing order," for "the sense of an alternative is freedom." It was just *that* sense the Christians experienced in their weekly worship of "the God and Father of our Lord Jesus Christ." Some "firemen," these Christians![7]

In this context, the most "spiritual" of the early church's activities —its liturgical hymns and prayers and sacraments—were its most political defiance of "the powers that be." Periodically for three centuries, it was not so much illegal to be a Christian as to "go to church." Do not "stay away from our meetings," said the writer of Hebrews. During all the periods of persecution, it was tempting indeed to stay home on rainy Sundays.

They encouraged one another to "keep the faith." In a sense, all the early Christians had to bind them together was an "idea." But what an idea: Now they were bit players in the "Divine Comedy," a life story that ended in joyful triumph rather than grim tragedy. To believe that, against all the accumulating evidences of tragedy in human experience; to believe it in face of disease, earthquakes, murder, hunger, injustice, infidelity, spite, and scorn—to believe that none of these things can "separate us from the love of God in Christ Jesus our Lord" was more than any lonely individual could manage. Jesus had said, "Where two or three have met together in my name, I am there among them." (Matt. 18:20.) Not to each Christian in the privacy of his or her self, this was a promise to the church as a community, which gathers that each member may be encouraged in the faith—not only to *keep* it but to *witness* to it. For example, sitting in a Roman prison, the apostle Paul writes a letter to the Christian church at Philippi. He draws encouragement from his knowledge that its members pray for him. He offers them encouragement in the knowledge that, even with six hundred miles between them, they share in a common struggle to tell the whole inhabited earth that Jesus is Lord:

> I thank my God whenever I think of you; and when I pray for you all, my prayers are always joyful, because of the part you have taken in the work of the Gospel from the first day until now. Of one thing I am certain: the One who started the good work in you will bring it to completion by the Day of Christ Jesus. It is indeed only right that I should feel like this about you all, because you hold me in such affection, and because, when I lie in prison or appear in the dock to vouch for the truth of the Gospel, you all share in the privilege that is mine. God knows how I long for you all, with the deep yearning of Christ Jesus himself. And this is my prayer, that your love may grow ever richer and richer in knowledge and insight of every kind, and may thus bring you the gift of true discrimination. . . .
>
> Yes, and rejoice I will, knowing well that the issue of it all will be my deliverance, because you are praying for me and the Spirit of Jesus Christ

is given me for support. For, as I passionately hope, I shall have no cause to be ashamed, but shall speak so boldly that now as always the greatness of Christ will shine out clearly in my person, whether through my life or through my death. For to me life is Christ, and death gain. . . .

Only, let your conduct be worthy of the gospel of Christ, so that whether I come and see you for myself or hear about you from a distance, I may know that you are standing firm, one in spirit, one in mind, contending as one man for the gospel faith, meeting your opponents without so much as a tremor. . . . You and I are engaged in the same contest; you saw me in it once, and, as you hear, I am in it still." (Phil. 1:2–9, 19–21, 27–28, 30)

By any measure, these are the words of a man speaking as a member of a remarkably close, mutually supportive human community. The early Christians shared a rare relationship only possible between persons who are sure that the meaning of life itself binds them together, and who are busy handing it swiftly on to others. They saw themselves as hungry people who had found food which was no joy to eat alone; and they felt bound to hand it on to as many others as wanted it. They were, in short, a revolutionary missionary fellowship, eager to help one another to remain strong in the faith that demanded always to be given away.

Supremely, then, they loved one another and the stranger. Old Testament prophets, we remember, had a rugged, visible test of genuine religion: "deal fairly with one another, do not oppress the alien, the orphan, and the widow, shed no innocent blood in this place" (Jer. 7:5–6). Amos thundered against people who "grind the heads of the poor into the earth and thrust the humble out of their way" (Amos 2:7). Adding very little to this old Hebrew ethic, Jesus said to his disciples simply that "hereby will all men know that you are my disciples, if you love one another" (John 13:35). It proved a historically accurate prediction. Non-Christians in the first century or two, we are told, observed the comings and goings of Christians and sometimes exclaimed: "Behold, how they love one another!" The data behind such an observation had to include something more remarkable than the affection that blood kin, husbands and wives, soldiers, and friends sometimes show to each other. *The remarkable feature of the early church community was the social diversity of its members.* Theirs was a religious fellowship that went out of its way to incorporate "the alien, the orphan, the widow," and others unaccustomed to associate with each other intimately in that day.[8]

An astounding example of this fellowship-in-the-process-of-becoming can be found in Acts 16:11–40. Here we see the beginning of the church at Philippi. Check this passage and you will find a strange list of persons who successively numbered themselves as Christians within a few days' time: several women, who in a male-dominated society were not the natural candidates for the first members of any important organization; one of them, Lydia, a successful merchant and a Gentile who had associated herself with the faith of Judaism; next, a woman of a radically different social class, a demented slave girl, who may not have become a member of the church but who benefited from Paul's care for her at great cost to him; next, a soldier in charge of putting up Paul and his companion Silas in the town jail overnight; and finally, the members of that jailer's family, including his children, who underwent baptism before the sun was up. This latter incident, we remember, took place under the auspices of two gospel preachers whose backs were bloodied by high-handed, illegal judicial proceedings that had put them in jail. Before this first Philippi sojourn was over, Paul fastened public blame on the officials who had made this mistake, so that the local citizens had good reason to exclaim: "Behold how they love one another and call our leaders to practice public justice!" Thus did an apostolic visit bring into being a young Christian congregation in Philippi: composed of women, children, and men who, prior to the visit, would not have thought of saying "hello" to one another on the street. No wonder that Paul and Silas at their next port of call were already known as people who had

> made trouble all over the world [and] have now come here. . . . They all flout the Emperor's laws and assert that there is a rival king, Jesus. (Acts 17:7)

The mixture of truth and exaggeration in this tribute tells us a lot about the revolutionary nature of the early church. Paul had demonstrated in Philippi that some of the "Emperor's laws," when obeyed, were vital to the protection of *Christians.* He had also imported into the town a *religio illicita* whose most illicit "trouble" was its quiet attack on social, economic, and political *status systems* of the local society.

Thus, in Philippi and increasingly all over the Roman Empire, the new Christian community quietly salted the social earth, invisibly leavened the social lump, and brought visible light to the dark corners of social injustice *chiefly by opening the doors of its membership to all levels of every local society.* To keep those doors open meant many a struggle with local social tradition, which only too often infiltrated the life of the Christian congregation itself. We know this from Paul's letter to the church in Corinth. There the gospel faith and the gospel ethic seemed not to root so quickly as in Philippi. As described by Paul in I Cor., ch. 11, the richer members of the church offended against the elemental principle of Christian unity by the simple rudeness of refusing to wait for all members to assemble before eating began. This selfish *individualization* of a mere "church supper" (or "love feast") was destroying the context, meaning, and reality of the climax of congregational worship, the Lord's Supper.[9] Whether through the positive example of Philippi or the negative one of Corinth, the human social reality struggling to be born in those early congregations of Christians constituted a revolutionary vision: establishing the ultimate equality of man and woman, feeding the starving, encouraging the hopeless, and giving the rootless a place to call home.

At its Spirit-filled best, the early church's social behavior had little in common with either a mere personal ethic or the ethic of an ingroup. The only ethics known to the Old and New Testaments is a social ethic, just as the only person described in both Testaments is a person-in-relationship with other persons. In Paul's "oikodomic (upbuilding) ethic" the rightness of any person's words and actions always must be judged, not by the lonely voice of "conscience," but by their upbuilding or downgrading effect upon one's neighbors. An individual Christian may be liberated for some exalted religious experiences such as "speaking in tongues," or liberated from many of the petty practices of both Gentile idolatry and Jewish law. But over all such personal freedom Paul wrote the great constraint: "Be careful that this liberty of yours does not become a pitfall for the weak." (I Cor. 8:9.) Christians are to remember the impact of their conduct upon the stranger, "The plain man . . . when he does not know what you are saying" (I Cor. 14:16). As Günther Bornkamm summarizes it: "The congregation as the 'body of Christ' is the place where the love of the Lord given in death is to be experienced, and therefore 'edification' in responsibility for the brethren is the only criterion by which even the 'gifts of the spirit' are to be judged, namely as gifts of grace and service."[10]

To strengthen, to build up, to offer a home: the Greek word *oikodomeō* in the New Testament carries all three meanings. The Christian community has been given in Jesus Christ and in his Spirit the power to practice an *ethic of relation-building*. Here is a unique society indeed, where the " 'life of the whole' is not secured at the expense of the parts."[11] The worshiping community provides "all who will" a home where they will be nurtured in faith, care, unity, and mission. Centuries later Augustine summarized it eloquently: "The low-spirited are to be encouraged, the infirm to be supported, objectors confuted, the treacherous guarded against, the unskilled taught, the lazy aroused, the contentious restrained, the haughty repressed, litigants pacified, the poor relieved, the oppressed liberated, the good approved, the evil borne with, and all are to be loved."[12]

Why? The answer was as simple for them as it was profound: "We love, because he first loved us." (I John 4:20.)

"We" in the New Testament account is a pronoun of drastic inclusiveness. No ingroup referent here, but a People of God whose structured group life constantly flings open windows and doors to the outside society of other people, equally worthy of being counted members of such a People. As Paul's example in Philippi demonstrates eloquently, concern for the oppressed and exploited people of society occurs among Christians along the roadside as they preach the gospel, in the courtrooms where faithful witness sometimes puts them, and in the jail where they sometimes reside alongside other victims of injustice. The home-giving community shapes a life of moving back and forth, to and from the homes of all humanity. *The upbuilding community exists for upbuilding the world,* as leaven exists for bread, salt for food, and light for the household.

From this New Testament picture we get a glimpse of what sort of intimate interchange between "personal" and "public" human life must be achieved if we humans are to enjoy *one* life that is simultaneously personal, interpersonal, and public. How these several dimensions of the human came to be separated in modern culture will be the subject of the next chapter.

Chapter 4

"A City
Set on a Hill"

Some theories of Bible interpretation lead us to believe that the word of God hurtles, like a rocket, out of the first century A.D. into the twentieth, neither scratched nor polished by the handing-on processes of the intervening centuries. The image is untenable all around. Every Christian in the world has learned to speak the language of the faith in the accent of his or her immediate ancestors. Debate over the meaning of the message in the church often roots in differences between those ancestors. And one reason we go back to the Bible is to distinguish, if we can, between the meaning of the message to Jeremiah, to Paul, to various intervening ancestors, and its meaning now to us. To make these distinctions is not to eliminate any one of the several lenses through which we discern the message in our own times. To the contrary: When we know how history has *both* scratched and polished our understanding, how our immediate ancestors have both highlighted and obscured the message of our more remote ancestors, we are better equipped to learn from both of them. And consciously or otherwise, we will put our own imprint upon the message as it passes from our hands to the hands of our descendants.

In this chapter we seek to identify several dimensions of Biblical faith and ethics which have been either highlighted or obscured for American Protestant Christians, as they have asked and answered the ancient questions of the Old Testament prophets:

Is it possible to build a city where God is worshiped truly and where citizens deal with one another justly and mercifully?

American Protestants have answered with their own particular blend of "yes" and "no." The purpose of this chapter is to detect the accent, the slant, and the perspective that shaped the answer. The chapter will probe history too briefly to suit the professional historians, but better a few searchlights into our past than none at all. Against a much-quoted word of the American industrialist Henry Ford—"History is bunk"—stands the word of American novelist William Faulkner—"The past is not dead; it isn't even past."

From Jerusalem to Rome

As we have seen, early Jews and Christians experienced much *ambivalence* toward particular cities in their history. Some cities in the Bible command little but contempt from those who write about them: Sodom, Pithom, Nineveh, Babylon. Yet even of these cities we find some positive religious affirmations. Abraham prays for the "righteous" citizens of Sodom (Gen. 18:23–33). God commands Jonah to preach forgiveness and repentance to Nineveh. Jeremiah advises the Jewish captives to settle down in Babylon and to "pray for the welfare of the city." For all its cruelties, Babylon remains an instrument of the Lord's just rule over the world.

Of at least one city, prophetic ambivalence was clearly poised between positive and negative stances: Jerusalem is center stage in the drama of history. All the prophets believed that, including the prophet from Nazareth, who said sorrowfully, "It is unthinkable for a prophet to meet his death anywhere but in Jerusalem." (Luke 13:33.) But he loved the city deeply enough to weep over it:

> O Jerusalem, Jerusalem, the city that murders the prophets and stones the messengers sent to her! How often have I longed to gather your children, as a hen gathers her brood under her wings; but you would not let me. Look, look! there is your temple, forsaken by God. (Matt. 23:37–38)

> If only you had known, on this great day, the way that leads to peace! But no; it is hidden from your sight. For a time will come upon you, when your enemies will set up siege-works against you; they will encircle you and hem you in at every point; they will bring you to the ground, you and your children within your walls, and not leave you one stone standing on another, because you did not recognize God's moment when it came. (Luke 19:41–44)

This prediction of Jesus was fulfilled several decades later. Second-generation Christians collected the writings that became the New Testament in the shadow of a terrible memory, the devastation of Jerusalem by the Roman legions of Hadrian in A.D. 70. Their spiritual assessment of Jerusalem and Rome was unforgettably expressed in the book of Revelation. There, from his exile on the Isle of Patmos, John reasserted the eminence of Jerusalem in world history by naming the "new heaven and new earth" after that city! He also reasserted the conviction of many Jews and Christians that world evil concentrated in world empires, for which "Babylon" remained an accurate symbol. In all probability John's identification of the demonic powers as "Babylon" is his thin disguise for "Rome," the latest greatest idolater, killer of saints, and perpetrator of oppression. No ambivalence toward Rome in Revelation: continued utter contempt.

The writing of the apostle Paul, however, retained the old prophetic ambivalence toward Jerusalem and extended the same to Rome. Paul held out a hand toward Rome that may have perplexed Jewish and Gentile Christians of his day. He openly boasts of his own Roman citizenship (Acts 21:39); he uses Roman law to achieve a modicum of justice for himself and his fellows (Acts 16:37; 22:25); and, most remarkably, he wants so much to preach the gospel in Rome before he dies that he "appeals to Caesar" to arbitrate his legal entanglement with the Roman and Jewish authorities in Judaea (Acts 25:11). Nowhere in the writings of Paul do we find him praying what John, in effect, prayed about Rome from Patmos: "*Écrasez l'infâme!*" ("Crush the vile thing!") Should Rome be crushed? Infamous as some of its policies were, much was humanly beneficial. Without the imperial legal structure, its roads and commerce, its perforating of tribal frontiers, how would the gospel get preached, by Jesus' own intention, "away to the ends of the earth" (Acts 1:8)? Paul seemed to say: Let Rome be. Her emperors are wrong to ask for the worship of Christians. But God can use this Empire for his purposes, as he used others.

To take a long leap into later history it is ironic to note that the French words above from the lips of Voltaire were directed against the Christian church of his time. Over a millennium and a half, what happened to the Christian movement that would give the least provocation to such an execratory "prayer" by the famous deistic philosopher?

Anyone's answer to that question will bear the marks of the writer's own slant on two thousand years of European history. American Protestant Christians dwell admiringly upon those New Testament congregations spread around the cities of the Roman Empire, because we image ourselves as thus spread around the cities of the United States. We see our Protestant history (since 1517) as a struggle against the compromises and degradations imposed on the Christian movement by Emperor Constantine's courtship of the Christian church in A.D. 312 and Emperor Theodosius' marriage of the Empire to the church soon thereafter. What an inconceivable turnabout! By A.D. 380 Christianity was the *only* "legal religion" for people living inside the Roman Empire. Now it was illegal to be anything else *but* a Christian.[1]

We will understand those remote generations of Christians better if we consider the audience to which Augustine wrote his book, *The City of God,* in the fifth century. Rome's toleration for Christians of the fourth century coincided with a profound political crisis in the Empire itself. Now the Empire was falling apart. Only 10 percent of the population may have had some connection with the Christian church; but the Christian movement was apparently the most vigorous religion around. Whatever the motive behind Emperor Constantine's conversion, the level of political disorder in his empire was high. It plainly stood in need of new religious "glue" to supplant the old emperor worship. Moving his capital to Constantinople, he demoted the city of Rome to second-class political status. As Theodosius was opening church doors to everyone, barbarians were banging on the gates of the old city. In A.D. 410 they sacked it and left behind many a visible sign that the thousand years of Rome were at an end. In the western part of the Empire, law and order were crumbling.

Thus, the audience to which Augustine wrote *The City of God* was a mixture of fifteenth- and first-generation Christians, most of whom suffered great personal anxiety in face of the political decay around them. The gist of his great book was in its title. Christians have never had a "continuing city" on earth. Our home is certainly not in Eternal Rome, whose rulers made the mistake of assuming eternity for themselves. In the name of Jesus, we worship the Eternal, we have a permanent "City" in him alone. Here on earth we are only pilgrims. But we are not lonely pilgrims. We enjoy the presence of God in this world, which he rules and Rome never did rule. We enjoy community with one another in our common love for him. There are in fact *two cities,* two communities of human beings, in this world. History consists in the mixture and the conflict of the two communities. One, typified by Rome, rests on the shaky foundation of pride and love of self; the other, typified by the church, rests on the firm foundation of humility and love of neighbor. Be thankful if you can count yourself a citizen of both cities while knowing the superior worth of the *civitas Dei* over the *civitas mundi!*[2]

The Augustinian vision amounted to a new, robust world view that both undermined the Roman political order and reset that order on new foundations. *Dethroned forever were the pretensions of government to divinity.* Set up anew was Christian membership in a Kingdom that embraced all humanity, "barbarian" and "cultured" people alike. *Therefore Christians were now free to be political without being idolatrous.* As Charles Cochrane puts it, Christians no longer had to see themselves as "moral men" in an "immoral society." Now a society governed by the principle of love for God and all people was at least conceivable. The church itself was forerunner of such a society.

> Instead of the "semblance and shadow of peace" precariously ensured by secularism, [the new society] embodies the substance of a peace exhibiting the fullest measure of order and concord possible in human beings, the peace of an association whose members "enjoy God and one another in God." To this peace they pledge themselves in a new oath or sacrament . . . a sacrament conceived, not as an act of self-surrender analogous to that whereby the citizen of this world resigns his will into the keeping of a temporal sovereign, but rather as a covenant of emancipation from temporality, mutually undertaken by men who thus profess themselves aliens from secularism. It is a testament, not of subjection to, but of salvation from, the divinity of Caesar, mystically proclaimed through baptism in the name of the Father, the Son, and the Holy Spirit. At the same time it is a vow of unyielding opposition to all who deny or reject

the claims of the Evangel. In this opposition Christianity finds the true logic of the *saeculum,* the hand of God in human history.[3]

In the same century when the great theologian characterized the whole of history as "a tale of two cities," the church was settling many practical questions about its own proliferating organization. With everyone around the Mediterranean basin now officially Christian, church affairs involved society-wide affairs. With old imperial structures collapsing, the church, through bishops like Augustine, was in some locales the strongest enforcer of law and order. Then came the beginning of another movement whose leaders united around this intriguing idea: Let us fill the growing vacuum of political power in the city of Rome with the growing prestige of the earthly representatives of the *civitas Dei.* Let New Rome rise on the ashes of the old. Let the old heart of the Empire become the new heart of the church. Let the Bishop of Rome model the structures of the worldwide church on the structures of the fading empire. Let Christians have *their* Jerusalem: Holy Rome!

We misread this crucial century of church history if we neglect to notice the large number of "protestants" who objected to the new imperial church. Great numbers of Christians now fled the civilized church for monasteries in the desert, where a less compromised version of the Christian life might be practiced. Groups of radical puritans such as the Donatists in North Africa sought to distinguish between the committed and the accommodated styles of Christian discipleship. In his own struggle to keep this particular sect united with the church, Bishop Augustine came finally to a momentous rule: To be rightly related to the church of Christ, one had to be submissive to the will of one's local bishop. By an easy development of ecclesiology, that rule eventually came to read: To relate rightly to the church, one has to be rightly related to the Bishop of Rome. The idea of the papacy was beginning to flower.

Any organization of people is likely to have public consequence. In the western portion of the old Empire, the organizational church intertwined with the total organization of society. In the Dark Ages (the fifth to the eleventh centuries) the church became the *only* structure that linked Germans and Italians, Franks and Anglo-Saxons, Spaniards and Norsemen into one human social structure. Medieval feudalism slowly developed. It was an agrarian society, controlled by lords-of-land with peasant serfs whose slavelike station the church came to assign to the will of God. Indeed it came to baptize the whole medieval social structure as the God-ordained pattern for the earthly human city. Society and church developed their hierarchies simultaneously. Through alliances of political and ecclesiastical princes, religion and politics mixed intimately.[4]

One crucial generalization must be made about the church-state relations of the thousand years of European history which Augustine's vision helped to shape. On very few occasions did either a political or a church official succeed long in nullifying the power of the other. In ancient Rome the emperor claimed to be a god, and no one officially contradicted him. The New Rome of the church was a standing contradiction to any equivalent claim by feudal lords. "The sword of the state" had always over against it "the sword of the Spirit" wielded by the church. Instances of church-sponsored revolt against the feudal system were few indeed. With its financial support and social prestige interlocked with that system, what could such revolt be but revolt against itself? At the same time, both the theology and the organization of the medieval church required a separation of church and state as old as Jeremiah. One remembers Pope Gregory's power to make Henry IV of Germany cool his heels outside in the snow at Canossa and Thomas à Becket's ultimate vindication over his murderer Henry II of England. The church also asserted its right to enforce its own laws for clergy, and the "right of sanctuary" whereby a hapless fugitive could find a place of safekeeping inside a church building. In these and other ways, the church of the medieval era showed a degree of independence from political structures. In this fact, and in the theology underlying it, lay buried other seeds of change.

FROM ROME TO GENEVA

In pockets of its own life, sometimes against the intentions of its high officials, the church nourished in certain spirits a vision of "a better city" than feudal church and society embodied. Illustrations came most often from the monastery, that safety valve for radical Christians tired of the prevailing spiritual compromise. More than others, the monastics saw themselves as pilgrim followers of Jesus "outside the camp" of conformist church life. Again and again, they recalled the church to standards of worship, justice, and mercy which accommodating Christians neglected. Again and again, reform fell short. The "better city" of Heb., chs. 11 and 13, seemed permanently hidden in the mists of God's still-future Kingdom.

The most eloquent example of such a spirit was Francis of Assisi, thirteenth-century founder of the monastic order that bears his name. For at least eight hundred years, medieval society had been a network of rural, agricultural villages. Many cities of the time were really small towns. Even Rome was no large city by twentieth-century standards. With the Crusades and other international events of the eleventh and following centuries, however, commerce began to stir across feudal borders. Shipping and overland transportation developed. A strange new class of tradespeople, neither aristocrat nor serf, took up residence around the old walled towns. The "middle class" was getting born, and with it centers of commerce that were cities indeed.

Identified so closely with the dispersed, feudal society, the church had long ago settled down as an organization of country churches. Parish priests went about their work in the villages, and monasteries dotted the landscape on roomy tracts that made them feudal powers in their own right. Then came the urban migration. As so often in human history, the success of one generation lays the groundwork of the failure of the next. Its missionary troops spread out over the countryside, the church had few left over for the ministry to the mushrooming cities of Italy and France. The priests were in the country; the monks were in the country; but the cities were filling up with people in need of food, sick care, weekly Mass, or the preaching of the gospel. Would anybody see the cities as a new, internal missionary field? The middle-class youth from Assisi, inspired by love of Jesus to imitate "Lady Poverty," answered "yes" to this need. He and his followers tramped the streets of Padua, Milan, Venice, Florence, and Rome itself, scattering bread, kind words, medicine, the Sacrament, and other acts of charity. It was a belated demonstration that the love of Jesus, in the power of the Spirit, followed people into cities too. Then what Francis became to urban charity, Dominic became to urban preaching. The two orders named after them pioneered the church's presence in the new commercial cities. They were Europe's first City Missionary Societies.

Europe's future for the next several centuries was being shaped in these new cities. In concert with urban tradespeople kings levied taxes and recruited armies to build the political form that would dominate the world into our own time: the nation-state. By the fifteenth century, kings of France, England, and Spain were proudly warring on one another, having established their supremacy over their own feudal nobility. In these struggles the leaders of the church were caught in a difficult position. Nationalism was breaking up the loosely hinged feudal system and the continental church as well. In a war between England and France, with whom would the pope side? Increasingly, the pope's answer made little difference. As a political power, the papacy began to decline.

In the midst of all this ferment, the spiritual power of the church confronted another challenge, again from the direction of the monastery. The monk this time was Martin Luther, and his initial tool of protest was his study of the Bible. Indeed, for most Protestants, "real" church history begins right here, fifteen hundred years into the Christian Era. It is natural for us to feel that Luther fought *our* battle when he asserted the supreme authority of Scripture, struggled with *us* to achieve a relation to God as direct and simple as that of Christians in ancient Philippi, and restored to *us* the equality of Christian believers as "priests." What a majority of American Protestant Christians believe about themselves presupposes the Lutheran Reformation.

But Luther was born before Columbus set sail from Cadiz. His influence on the Christian movement in America was to be mediated by a Frenchman, John Calvin, a second-generation reformer converted to Lutheranism about 1533. Like Luther, Calvin's career was fundamentally shaped by the new national politics of his time. Unlike Luther, he was not lucky enough to incur the protection of a friendly local monarch after his break with Catholicism. Pursued by hostile church and government officials in France, he took a hasty departure for Switzerland in the year 1536. His life as a reformer came to concentrate in the single city of Geneva. Because he became the Protestant theologian who most influenced the earliest white settlers of eastern North America, Calvin's twenty-five-year ministry in Geneva touched modern American history in powerful ways.[5]

Calvin was fortunate to have Geneva as his arena of reform. An independent city, with a population of some twelve thousand in 1536, Geneva had aristocrats but no king. Its church leaders had declared themselves free of the pope's jurisdiction. But, like true medievalists, they expected government to participate in the reform of the church. One of Calvin's contributions to Geneva was his like insistence that the church participate in the reform of government. In keeping with his own principle that "the Christian must know that during his whole life he has to do with God," Calvin's religious view of the world impelled him to leave nothing untouched by the reformer's eye. He read the Bible as calling for unceasing reformation of the human under the guidance of the divine Spirit. In Geneva, individuals, groups, the city itself would discover that their whole life "had to do with God." More than any other branch of the Reformation (said Ernst Troeltsch) Calvinists thus began their search for a "Holy Community"—an ecclesiastical-civil way of life that squared in all respects with a diligent reading of the Bible.[6]

Calvin found in the New Testament the promise of a human relation to God at once personal and social. The direct access of the believer to the Bible had as its precedent the direct access of the disciples to Jesus. Rather than depend upon priests and sacraments for assurance of the grace of God, the Christian could have that assurance directly through the Scripture under the guidance of the Spirit. To Calvin the fellowship of the church remained vital for the personal Christian life; but the individual, the church, and civil society were all radically dependent upon God. In place of graded levels of Christian commitment represented in medieval Catholicism by monk, secular priest, and layperson, Calvinists saw the whole of the human community "level" before God. All of life became subject to the same "unremitting measure" of the ever-active divine will. The result, to use a famous phrase by the sociologist Max Weber, was the restoration of an ideal of *strenuous* discipleship—"this-worldly asceticism."[7] In a sense that the prophets of the Old Testament would have appreciated, Calvin believed that the world is "the theater of God's glory." He called every Christian to act onstage in the conviction that his or her part was crucial to the completion of the divine drama.

Calvin's own part in the drama was that of a parish minister. Only late in his life did city officials grant him citizenship. In all other respects Calvin was "preacher to the city" as well as preacher to a Sunday congregation. A week in Calvin's ministry was as likely to include an argument with local merchants over interest rates as a discussion with church elders over the proper form of the Communion service. He was as likely to be seen in a meeting of the town council seeking to change the civil-dominated system for electing church leaders as in his own study at night writing Bible commentaries. And he was as likely to be discussing with a manufacturer a scheme for getting jobs for unemployed Protestant refugees as he was to be preparing next Sunday's sermon. Like few other church reformers in history, Calvin crisscrossed the boundaries between "personal" and "social" religious concern, between church politics and civil politics, between the sacred and the secular. Just how pervasively involved he became in the whole life of Geneva is vividly expressed in this paragraph from the historian John T. McNeill:

> After the 1557 elections syndics [town council] ordered a reforming visitation of the city. Servants were to be admonished to attend church, and parents to send their children to school. Nurses of babies were warned not to go to bed with them. Rascals and scoundrels were to be arrested. No fires were to be permitted in rooms without chimneys, and chimneys were to be swept for safety. Latrines were to be provided for houses in which they were lacking, and the streets kept clean. Rooms were not to be let without police permission; and the night watch was to be duly performed by those appointed or by reliable substitutes. Such matters came within Calvin's care. He was also asked to sit in judgment on an invention for the cheaper heating of houses and on a painting to commemorate the peace with Bern. It was at his suggestion that railings were ordered for the balconies of houses for the safety of children, and it was he who brought about strict enforcement of the law against recruiting mercenaries in Geneva. He also, as early as December 1544, prompted

the Little Council to introduce the manufacture of cloth in order to provide a livelihood for the unemployed poor. The first dentist who appeared in Geneva was not licensed until Calvin had personally tested his skill. Dishonest or exorbitant practices in business were severely penalized.[8]

Clearly Calvin had an "ethic of upbuilding" whose social scope was more comprehensive than the one which the apostle Paul could urge upon his young churches. Not just spasmodically, as in Philippi, but systematically, as in Geneva, Christians were to subject the whole of human life to the will of God. Fundamental to this Christian life-style was the perpetual link between personal and social discipleship. We are, says Calvin in echo of Paul, "chiefly to study our neighbor's advantage. No increase is advantageous unless it answers to the needs of the whole body. . . . Let not man be anything for himself, but let us all be whatever we are for each other."[9]

Calvin's contribution to the *economics* of Geneva deserves our careful attention. Scholars like Weber claim that Calvin influenced the New World especially in the economic realm. His intense interest in manufacturing in Geneva came partly from his sense that the Biblical demand of "justice for the poor" called for hard work, simple living, and generosity. Calvin died a poor man in the city he helped make richer. His capacity for self-denial—"to the greater glory of God"—achieved poignant expression in his instruction to his family to bury him without a grave marker. Thirty days after his death no one in Geneva knew just where his body lay. Reproduced in his most faithful followers, this capacity for self-denial—"delayed gratification" as a modern psychologist would say—had enormous impact upon the economic life of Europe and America over the next two hundred years.

Again, as so often in history, the intentions of one generation of reformers get curiously reshaped by subsequent generations. If Max Weber was right about the connection between "The Protestant Ethic and the Spirit of Capitalism," the reshaping went like this:

In their original conversion to the Protestant Reformation, the merchants of Geneva had political-economic as well as theological interest. Geneva was a free city, which buttressed its civil liberty with the increasing liberty of its economic transactions in an expanding

European market. Prior to Calvin's coming, Geneva was famous for two industries: prostitution and banking. Calvin's reform destroyed much of the first but merely regulated the second. The idea of interest on money was acceptable to him, in contrast to the official church prohibition of usury during the Middle Ages. Genevan bankers had been borrowing and lending money with interest for years; but Calvin insisted upon restraining personal accumulation of wealth and setting interest rates with an eye to "the needs of the whole body" of the Genevan citizenry.[10] He appreciated the power of Geneva's commercial wealth to protect the city's independence from the French king and other political predators. Further, in the newly invented commercial corporation he saw a way to multiply wealth by social cooperation which individual farming and trading could not equal.

For many centuries the economic system in Europe had been static. The amount and value of life-sustaining products stayed the same from generation to generation, or so most people believed. The new capitalism, however, assumed that economics was not a "zero sum" game in which a fixed volume of wealth circulates among all the players. Production and distribution can become a "positive sum" enterprise in which each person makes an investment and takes out only so much as the success of the enterprise permits. In a relatively small community like Geneva, the relation between the individual investor, the stock corporation, and the entire community could be known, scrutinized, and regulated. The participants in the economic system shared a common understanding of the difference between just and unjust interest rates, necessary and luxurious consumption, good and bad objects of investment. But there were forces in the economy and in the Reformation that would soon erode this consensus. On the one hand, money is a remarkably impersonal human invention. It can easily get detached from its possessor by being invested five hundred miles away. When money "escapes" across political frontiers, who can control how it may be used? Suppose one seeks to make more money than any controller is likely to permit. Suppose further that a newfound sense of personal accountability to God alone pervades the investor. He is a good Calvinist believing that economic activity, as well as prayer, glorifies God. Far from being a sin, the accumulation of wealth can be virtuous. If the accumulator has worked hard, bought wisely, sold honestly, avoided luxury, cultivated generosity, and steadfastly resisted the *spirit* of greed and mammon worship, he has become a self-conscious, independent-minded individual. He has not had much time to subject his business to the scrutiny of neighbors in the church or the community. If they too "mind their own business," they will be just as preoccupied. The personal discipline of buying and selling in an increasingly impersonal market overwhelms the remnants of a social discipline upon individual accumulators.

Described this way, the "Protestant ethic" is highly compatible with the emerging "spirit of capitalism." One might put it baldly: As Protestantism tended toward private enterprise in religion, capitalism tended toward private enterprise in economics. Once the idea of dynamic progress had succeeded in either area, the spirit of active innovation was reinforced in the other area. In this theory Calvin and the other Reformers were not the cause of capitalism in Western Europe; rather, the two movements now and again fortified each other. Protestantism never developed a systematic theory of economics. What it did produce was what might be called the "Protestant personality type." John T. McNeill gives us a keen insight into the personality pattern that Calvin set in his own self-discipline:

> Having early acquired the most exacting habits of work, he had no free boyhood and later gave himself very little time for recreation. Though he theoretically . . . approved of laughter . . . he made an asceticism of his labor and his proud refusal of ease. . . . He eloquently extols the Creator's handwork in the stars above and in the earth beneath, but shows little evidence of having paused to enjoy them. He praises the view from a house which he is providing for a friend, but does not mention the thrilling mountain scene from his own window. Those who blame him for all this are expecting a great deal of a sixteenth century man, and especially of an emaciated invalid with a continent's religious problems on his shoulders.[11]

Four centuries later, we have to conclude that these psychological contradictions proved the Achilles' heel in Calvin's attempt to bind the values of individual striving and community responsibility into a

single ethic for one communal life. The burden of holding all the
poles together—the *ethical* poles of personal and social responsibility,
the *economic* poles of individual and collective striving for wealth,
the *political* poles of free persons and free communities, and the
religious poles of personal faith and corporate church—proved too
much for most Protestants to bear.

The attempt was made, however, by third-generation Calvinists
who settled parts of the New World. In the seventeenth century,
people left Europe for many reasons. A group of English people called
Puritans left for reasons growing directly out of their Calvinism.

FROM GENEVA TO BOSTON

Soon after his death, Calvin's experiment in Christian urban
reform faltered. The connections of church life, civic politics, and
economic life in Geneva deteriorated. No longer did Protestants
think of Geneva, as John Knox did, as "the most perfect school of
Christ under heaven," a sort of Protestant Rome. Nevertheless, the
hunger for comprehensive religious-political reform lay deep in
Calvinists. Nowhere did they seek more earnestly to "purify" church
and the civil communities than in England and Scotland. That two-
sided search—for pure worship in the church and pure distinctions
between kings and The King erupted eventually in the English Civil
War of the 1640's.

A decade before that war, a group of Puritans under John Winthrop set sail for another, newer England. Discouraged by their
attempts to reform English church and society according to their
Calvinistic inclination, they determined to form their own society on
the coast of a continent that seemed a providential replication of
Israel's Promised Land. Though their self-confidence may shock us
now, the Puritans saw themselves as standing in a long line of emi-
grant-pilgrims from Moses to Jeremiah to Paul to Augustine to Calvin. They believed that prior to the heavenly city, God had an earthly
"city ready for them" (Heb. 11:16) if they had the courage to help
build it.

Seldom has any group of emigrants had their purposes so clearly
summarized as the Puritans in a sermon preached by their leader

John Winthrop aboard their ship, the *Arbella,* some days before it touched the New England coast. This document has become the epitome of the vision that lured the Massachusetts Bay colonists away from the corruptions of Europe. Winthrop begins by affirming the dependence of all people upon God their creator and upon one another in human society. No person has a special claim upon God's gifts, but by his own "providence" God has "ranked" society "into two sorts" of people—"rich and poor." Both mercy and justice must govern the relationships of the more and less favored people of society. Basic to the new purified civil community must be the commitment of each person to the welfare of others, both in the church and in the civil community. "The bond of love" is the first source of society:

We are a Company professing ourselves fellow members of Christ, in which respect only though we were absent from each other many miles, and had our employments as far distant, yet we ought to account ourselves knit together by this bond of love, and live in the exercise of it, if we would have comfort or our being in Christ. . . .

For the work we have in hand, it is by a mutual consent through a special overruling providence, and a more than an ordinary approbation of the Churches of Christ to seek out a place of Cohabitation and Consortship under a due form of Government both civil and ecclesiastical. In such cases as this the care of the public must oversway all private respects, by which not only conscience, but mere Civil policy doth bind us; for it is a true rule that particular estates cannot subsist in the ruin of the public. . . .

Now the only way to avoid this shipwreck and to provide for our posterity is to follow the Counsel of Micah, to do Justly, to love mercy, to walk humbly with our God, for this end, we must be knit together in this work as one man, we must entertain each other in brotherly Affection, we must be willing to abridge ourselves of our superfluities, for the supply of others' necessities, we must uphold a familiar Commerce together in all meekness, gentleness, patience and liberality, we must delight in each other, make others' Conditions our own, rejoice together, mourn together, labour, and suffer together, always having before our eyes our Commission and Community in the work, our community as members of the same body, so shall we keep the unity of the spirit in the bond of peace, the Lord will be our God and delight to dwell among us, as his own people and will commend a blessing upon us in all our ways, so that we shall see much more of his wisdom, power, goodness, and truth than formerly we have been acquainted with, we shall find that the God of Israel is among us, when ten of us shall be able to resist a thousand of our enemies, when he shall make us a praise and glory, that men shall say of succeeding plantations: the Lord make it like that of New England: for we must consider that we shall be as a City upon a Hill, the eyes of all people are upon us.[12]

Here, bundled together, are the fibers of Puritan social philosophy which Winthrop and his associates intended to weave into the fabric of the ideal Christian community: strict accountability of every person to God and to one another; commitment to the welfare of the community as well as the prosperity of the individual; the affirmation of wealth as a blessing of God, distributed unevenly in the community according to the unevenness of individual work and virtue; the expectation of special individual and collective effort by this community to build an exemplary "town on a hill" (Matt. 5:14) because God expects more from communities specially favored by him.

All these elements the Puritans conceived as bound together in a *covenant* between persons belonging to the church and civil communities. Ten years before, William Bradford and his smaller company of "pilgrims" had preceded them to New England. They too had come with the notion of building a society on the foundation of mutual, covenanting consent.

With the notion of the communal covenant the Puritan New Englanders combined the idea of private property. Of all the concepts imported into the New World, this one, perhaps, was destined to have the vastest influence. From the ancient landholding system of the Middle Ages, as well as from the marketplaces of Geneva and London, they had learned that human dignity and liberty depend upon the owning of property. Good Calvinists that they were, they insisted that property alone was not sufficient reason to make the long journey across the Atlantic. But the abundance of land on this continent beckoned them as deliverance from the injustices of English society. Here on a sparsely populated continent every ambitious farmer could be a landowner. Though none would be allowed by the community to own land without limit, the parceling out of land was for them the community's primary way of doing justice to the material needs of its members.

By general agreement with a minimum of formal government decision, the community had a say in what land each citizen would occupy. In a striking way, therefore, they believed in town-planning. Indeed, urban historian Sam Bass Warner describes these early New England towns as "the most completely planned of any American settlement" of the next three centuries.

> Puritan folk planning flourished along the Atlantic coast from Maine to Long Island a century before what is now the United States had a town large enough to be defined as a city. For a generation or two, medieval English village traditions fused with religious ideology to create a consensus concerning the religious, social, economic, and political framework for a good life. Each of the several hundred villages repeated a basic pattern. . . . They carried in their heads the specifications for a good life and a decent community, and for a time they were able to realize them.[13]

They believed that the "specifications" were permanently and timelessly good—a certainty that left them poorly equipped to deal with unexpected change.

> The relationships among men, the laws and customs of the village, the pursuit of agriculture and the trades, the reading of the Bible and the gathering of the congregation to hear the preaching of the ministry—all these, they thought, would permanently maintain their earthly segment of a divine universe.[14]

As the number of villages multiplied, land grants were made by the colonial legislature to clusters of new immigrant families—"free except for surveying costs and sometimes a purchase payment to the Indians." The heads of these families signed a covenant, and in subsequent deliberation decided on the size of the land parcels. Large families got large parcels; bachelors got small ones. The community's need for specific services might dictate a larger offer of land to a blacksmith, a carpenter, or a minister. "Finally, because as seventeenth-century Englishmen and Puritans the settlers recognized hierarchy to be the natural and desirable order of society, men of means or status were given larger allocations." Yet, says Warner:

Despite such differentials, most families in fact received very similar parcels, and with few exceptions the largest grants were not more than eight times the smallest. In Boston the wealthy grasped much more of the town's wealth in their hands. By all later American standards these first townships were the most equitable allocations of resources the country ever knew. A rough commonality of property prevailed, and no one was left out. Never again was popular consensus able to forge so inclusive and equitable an economic program. . . .

The genius of the township system . . . lay in its crude organization of freedom and opportunity in group, not individual, terms. More strongly than in the tightest urban ethnic or racial ghetto or in the closed union or in the inbred family corporation, the unity of land control combined with a common village and religious experience to force men of the time to seek change only in group terms.[15]

For all their effort to build their towns and their lives around a social covenant, Warner adds, the century-old Calvinist commitment to individualized effort was equally vigorous: "At the core of New England farming—as of New England religion—lay individual effort and responsibility."[16] Unfortunately this ethic of personal responsibility proved easier to pass on to children and grandchildren than the ethic of corporate accountability. To be a Puritan was to interweave one's personal affairs with the affairs of a neighbor; but one could be a "Yankee trader" on grounds of purely individualistic economic ambition.

The early Puritan settlers of America made great effort to control that ambition. R. H. Tawney tells of the legal prosecution endured in 1644 by one Robert Keane, "an ancient professor of the gospel, a man of eminent parts, wealthy and having but one child, having come over for conscience' sake and for the advancement of the gospel." But he got caught in the toils of Boston law for the crime of profit-making at the rate of sixpence on the shilling—50 percent interest. The court fined him two hundred pounds, a large amount for the time. But Mr. Keane was a Christian subject to church discipline, and a church meeting found him ready to "acknowledge his covetous and corrupt heart" before the elders. The incident provoked a Boston minister to denounce the notions "that a man might sell as dear as he can, and buy as cheap as he can" and "that he may sell as he bought, though he paid too dear."[17] Yet such were the very principles of market-determined economics which soon would erode the Calvinistic synthesis in New England.

At this same time began another erosion of the culture of Native Americans, now on collision course with white people's dreams. Nothing in the nature of land requires human beings to coin the notion of "real estate." How differently land could be viewed glimmers poignantly in the confusions which the "Indians" endured in their negotiations with Europeans over landownership. Exclaimed Tecumseh, chief of the Shawnee: "What! Sell land! As well sell air and water. The great spirit gave them in common to all, the air to breathe, the water to drink, and the land to live upon." And Chief Black Hawk related his brush with the new economics in the sad words: "I touched the goose quill to the treaty, not knowing, however, that, by that act, I consented to give away my village."[18]

Anything *real* may be *sold:* such was the tempting, simple maxim of the Yankee trader. A fundamental reason for "declension" of the Puritan into the Yankee was that others could emigrate from Europe to the New World on grounds of the same maxim.[19] With the spirit of capitalism on the upsurge on both sides of the Atlantic, wealth-hungry immigrants soon outnumbered the defenders of the old Puritan covenants. From the eighteenth century on, "going to America" meant "seeking one's fortune." The great cities of the Eastern seaboard—beginning with Boston and New York—were increasingly composed of individual fortune seekers. Perhaps no nation on earth had ever been so composed.

By a magnificent coincidence, a Scot named Adam Smith wrote a book in the birthday year of the United States of America which offered an economic theory that described eighteenth-century white American economic culture almost photographically. Individual economic striving is quite enough, said Smith, for anyone to concentrate on.

> By pursuing his own interest he frequently promotes that of the society more effectively than when he really intends to promote it. I have never known much good done by those who affected to trade for public good. It is an affectation.[20]

If one looks out for one's own economic good, what or who will look out for the good of "the community"? Never mind, said Smith; the market system, with all its individual competitors, has laws of its own. Each seeker of wealth

> is led by an invisible hand to promote an end which was not part of his intention.[21]

In his now-famous doctrine of the "invisible hand," Smith had invented a secularized version of the classic Christian faith in the sovereign God of history, paired with an equally secularized version of the responsible individual Christian. Economic accumulation, in this theory, becomes the chief daily pursuit of individual human beings. One may accumulate all the wealth one wishes in the benign certainty that the social good will somehow be served. Whether such an ethic should be called "Protestant" depends upon a reader's standards of historical judgment. It was surely a long way from either Paul's or Calvin's ethic of mutual upbuilding.

To CHICAGO AND WESTWARD

Except for those occasional social experiments represented among groups like the Mennonites and the Mormons, companies of religiously motivated immigrants seldom dared again to establish whole towns and cities in America. After the Puritans the theory and the practice of individualistic capitalism would account for the origin and growth of virtually every city on the American continent. From the coastal port cities of New York, Philadelphia, and Norfolk; to the inland river junctions of Cincinnati, St. Louis, Montreal, and New Orleans; to the wagon-train stops of Omaha, Denver, and Cheyenne; to the rail hubs of Chicago, Atlanta, Vancouver, and San Francisco —the cities of America mushroomed around nodes of commerce, transportation, and manufacturing. Exploding markets swelled in numbers to match the swelling hunger for wealth. The historical generalization is unavoidable: Urban America was built out of an abundance of popular desire and opportunity for riches.

If Adam Smith's philosophy played a dominant role in all this history, what part did the faith and the Christian churches continue to play? Though we do not aspire to give a detailed answer to that question here, we may summarize some basic answers of historians who have studied the churches of nineteenth-century America.[22]

During the first century of settlement, the perpetual inflow of immigrants to the Atlantic coast tended to erode the power of the established colonial churches, but their privileged position was not abolished until well after the Revolution. Legally the Congregational church was the established church of Massachusetts until 1833. By then, however, Jeffersonian "separation of church and state" had become a practical reality in most of the United States. Since early in the eighteenth century too many discrete religious communities —Anglicans, Presbyterians, Quakers, Baptists, Catholics—crowded into the country towns and the new cities to sustain a public claim that Calvin's Genevan partnership of church and state could be imitated in America. Each new religious group canceled out the privileged claims of the others. More strikingly: most eighteenth-century immigrants had little formal religious affiliation anyway. A majority of the signers of the Declaration of Independence would not have called themselves Christians. The first governmental census of 1790 gave evidence that not more than 10 percent of the citizens were members of churches. At the very moment when Voltaire's cry for the destruction of the established church of France was being realized in a revolution, the disestablished church was evolving as a fact of American life. Sometimes for opposite reasons, politicians and church leaders both applauded this evolution.

For the first time in western European history since Constantine, the "two swords" of church and state were *really* separated. Advocates of religious freedom, like the Baptist followers of Roger Williams, rejoiced in this return to the early church's freedom to worship without state interference. Advocates of government stripped of religious pretension, like the followers of Jefferson, as gladly barred the church from meddling in civil affairs. The step from "civil" to "economic" separation was short: the idea that the churches had any business meddling in business was equally suspect to many founders of the republic. Benjamin Franklin had congenial conversations with Adam Smith during several of his trips to Europe. A convert to Smith's economic individualism, Franklin fervently resisted the ancient corporate economic disciplines of the Bradfords and Winthrops in colonial history.

Numerically weak, divided in doctrine and organization, and excluded from formal governmental power, the churches of the young United States thus found themselves awkwardly related to their own past.

Many of the churches, especially those with a Calvinist heritage, still affirmed the classic connection between personal belief and public responsibility. Certain religious communities had taken vigorous part in the Revolution against England. In the mountain valleys of New York, Pennsylvania, and Virginia that conflict could even be called a "Presbyterian Revolution," so forcefully had the ministers of the region promoted the patriot cause from their pulpits. The first "Great Awakening"—the series of emotionally charged revivals that spread from colony to colony in the mid-eighteenth century—helped prepare the way for the Revolution, if only because the revivalists found themselves the leaders of a movement that spread quickly across colonial boundaries. But the new national constitution, with its Bill of Rights and firm prohibition against any national establishment of religion, deprived church leaders of any ready handles of political power. The independent mind of the entrepreneur, shared equally by prosperous eastern traders and their poor neighbors saddling horses to "go West," pushed religion out of the economic mainstream too. By the year 1800 the churches of America found themselves in a new world indeed. Having once seen themselves at the center of the new nation, they now felt strangely sidetracked in an unprecedented way. They lived in a Constantinian "settlement" (in that the official stance of the civil power was religious toleration) and in a post-Theodosian society as a minority institution without political privilege.

Reaction to the new situation was irregular and local during the early years of the republic. In the 1790's, out on the frontiers of New England and the Old Northwest, evangelists began to preach with little permission from their educated Eastern colleagues. New denominations emerged with their pioneer converts. Gradually the leaders of the coastal city churches—who had been quietly pondering their new minority status—awoke to their responsibility for promoting the "awakening" already in progress on the frontier. By the 1830's churches throughout the land were participating in some aspect of the new movement. For the shaping of Protestant consciousness in twentieth-century America, no event in the nineteenth century was to prove more important.

Like all historical events involving millions of people, the Second Great Awakening had too many results to be described simply. Church historians divide in their judgments on the questions, but their dominant conclusions run as follows:

Evangelism was the time-honored first mission of the Christian community; no reader of the New Testament had long to argue that. In this new land with its secular civil order and its religious freedom, the right of the churches to preach the gospel had firm protection. Foreign visitors to the United States in the early 1800's sometimes remarked on the popularity of religion that contrasted with the low popular percentage of members in the churches. The new Wesleyan Methodist circuit rider had already begun to follow the migration of unconverted people westward across the frontier. The time called for a mobile missionary church, not a church settled in Eastern villages. The United States was becoming continent-wide. A populous field waited to be harvested on the frontier and in the new cities. Into that field, therefore, the churches sent their missionary preachers. The evangelistic camp meeting and the riverside baptism were all part of the effort. Combined with a like impulse to preach the gospel in Africa and Asia, the "awakening" challenged the Protestant churches to an outpouring of energy that must be remembered as an astounding chapter in the history of the country.

How did the movement mobilize such energy? The same question could be asked of Paul and his followers in the Roman Empire. No doubt the Spirit moved in nineteenth-century America as in the first century for the upbuilding of the church. A remarkable, ambiguous feature of the Awakening, however, was its overt and covert relation to the social setting of mid-century America. During all the decades of camp meetings life-and-death questions of politics and economics were rocking the public life of the new country: the "irrepressible conflict" in the nation over the institution of slavery; the accumulation of power and wealth by people who saw the future economic growth of the country as tied to railroads, mechanical production, and cities; the continuing devastation of the first people to settle the continent—Indians; the first flexing of national muscle in an international war with Mexico; and the growing domination of government by people with large amounts of money to make or to keep. The sermons of the evangelists touched irregularly on these matters. Some converts understood their conversion as implicating them in reflection or action on such questions. In the 1830's and 1840's whole denominations underwent division over the issue of slavery. But many evangelists and their converts saw no connection between the gospel and abolitionism. While their predecessors in Jefferson and Franklin's time feared the intrusion of religion into politics and economics, many politicians and business leaders of mid-nineteenth-century America saw little to fear from these evangelists. In effect, says one historian, they said to the churches: "You stay within your narrowed sphere, and we will sanction you. Step out of it to discuss society's discontents; involve yourselves in the grand issue of slavery or oppose our wars or call into question our ways of arranging society, and we will destroy you."[23]

Seen from this side, the Second Great Awakening implied a new, informal contract for relating church and society in America. The good American citizen, the hardworking entrepreneur, and the good Christian were now one and the same person. The great westward movement could be described as conquering the West, as conquering poverty, or as conquering sin. The ground had now been laid for the puzzlement and anger, experienced by some twentieth-century American heirs to the Awakening, at the suggestion that personal Christian faith raises questions about such matters as *patriotism* and *wealth*. Insofar as personal faith does relate to American society, it related positively and enthusiastically.

On the connection between authentic Christian conversion and financial success, many preachers of the mid-1800's were eloquent. Not all of them were associated with revivalism. Indeed, often the loudest defenders of the "Gospel of Wealth" were pastors of rich established congregations whose members scorned the emotional excesses of revivalism. The Reverend Thomas P. Hunt, for example, argued in *The Book of Wealth* that "no man can be obedient to

God's will . . . without becoming wealthy." About 1850 Jonathan Mayhew Wainwright stated flatly:

> The unequal distribution of wealth we believe to be not only an unaltera-
> ble consequence of the nature of man, and the state of being in which
> he is placed, but also the only system by which his happiness and improve-
> ment can be promoted in this state of being.[24]

And on the eve of the Civil War, Marcus Wilson wrote in his *Second Reader* that schoolchildren "should be very thankful" that their "lot is better" than that of the urban poor, but they should not be proud. "It was God alone who made our lot to differ from the lot of theirs."[25] Wealth by this logic becomes a decided mark of God's blessing and approval of an individual. If God wills all to be rich, he wills none to be poor. If a person was poor, this was his own fault. Well into the twentieth century, the Reverend Russell Conwell of Philadelphia, in Chautauquas and other church meetings, assured millions of Americans that diamonds of economic opportunity lay buried in virtually every backyard:

> I say that you ought to get rich, and it is your duty to get rich.[26]

Some do their duty more faithfully than others; and some pages from Charles Darwin during these same years began to suggest a scientific explanation for this phenomenon. The drive for financial power and acquisition, the Darwinians claimed, is rooted in "nature." Wealth could give one the assurance that one was among the biologi-cally "fittest," if not among the religiously saved. Either way, seg-ments of the population that remained poor were suffering from their own unworthiness. The wealthy could not really be held accountable. Individual responsibility is the key to understanding the life situation of every human being. If certain groups seem to share a common poverty—as black, red, and yellow Americans did in the nineteenth century—they had only their laziness to thank.

But there was another side to the Second Great Awakening that continued the old vision of the Puritan "city upon a hill." As Timo-thy L. Smith has demonstrated, the opponents of revivalism were most often the leaders of Presbyterian, Episcopal, and Congrega-tional churches who had settled down in the securities of orthodox doctrine, wealth, and social prestige. A conservative Boston church publication of 1854, for example, compared the current revivalism unfavorably to the revivals of one hundred years before. The latter succeeded, he said, because they "drew a wide line between politics and religion, between the interests of this world and of another."[27] Such criticism came forth in reaction to that large number of gospel preachers in the 1850's who, says Smith, "defined carefully the relationship between personal salvation and community improvement and never tired of glowing descriptions of the social and economic millennium which they believed revival Christianity would bring into existence."[28] In a book that went through six editions in the mid-1850's, William Arthur, a leading Methodist "perfectionist," wrote of the two most dangerous perversions of the gospel: to look upon it as "a salvation for the soul after it leaves the body but no salvation from sin while there," and as "a means of forming a holy community in the world to come, but never in this." In the same book Arthur praised the "family feeling" which "glowed in the early Christian church" and still lived in Methodist testimony and class meetings. In those meetings, he said, Methodists were experiencing "the divine order of society."[29] Arthur's contemporary Charles G. Finney, the eminent revivalist of Oberlin, wrote a letter to ministers during the national election year of 1856. He invited them to inquire into the political beliefs of their parishioners "whether they are cleaving to a party without regard to principles," and "in what manner they demean themselves towards those who are in their employment."[30]

The effect of high or low wages could be most easily observed in the cities; and revival-motivated concern for industrial workers often flourished there. Preaching in Boston in 1842, evangelist Edward Norris Kirk denounced the view that poverty was God's punishment of indolence. Poverty may have a variety of causes. "When men love their neighbors as themselves, the causes of poverty will be sought out, and the remedy applied as far as possible." One possible aggravation of drunkenness among working people, he added, was the catering of the churches to the upper classes.[31] The next two decades saw small armies of Methodists, Baptists, Congregationalists, and revivalist Presbyterians recruited for work with poor people in the major Northern cities. Like modern-day Franciscans, they organized rooming houses, clothing shops, homes for unwed mothers, programs of assistance to prisoners, job searches for immigrants, industrial schools, and medical aid stations. Two years after Marcus Wilson had published his word to schoolchildren about the just deserts of the urban poor, Gilbert Haven—revivalist, Methodist, abolitionist—"warned his fellow clergymen that usury was as hard to preach against as slavery. 'Some rich brother, who has waxed fat on these ill-gotten gains will denounce you as an intermeddler, while his conduct uncensured, and himself undisciplined, keeps scores from the church.' "[32] It was the old Calvinist-Puritan theme that, two centuries before, had brought Robert Keane to belated repentance.

A similar, though more complicated, protest against slavery characterized this same group of revivalist leaders. Visiting the United States in 1858, the Frenchman Count Agénor de Gasparin concluded

> that the revival of 1858 had been a profound agitation of national conviction which had paved the way to the election of Lincoln. "The great moral force which is struggling with American slavery," he wrote, "is the Gospel."[33]

The society-reforming evangelicals thus stood out as that segment of Protestants most determined to preach a personal-social gospel to a nation about to experience an enormous outpouring of blood and treasure over the preservation of the national Union, the subsequent explosion of postwar industry, and the final conquest of the West. Having preached compassion for the poor as the fruit of conversion and structured social reform as the necessary anticipation of the coming Kingdom of Christ, the evangelical movement thus had a part, says Smith, in preparing the way for

> what came to be called the social gospel. The triumph of Yankee arms restored the faith of even Princeton conservatives that Christianity and civilization were marching forward toward perfection. Gilbert Haven, who had been Methodism's most notable abolitionist, predicted that the grace of Christ would "renew the land in holiness and love," halt the sale of alcoholic beverages, end the "luxurious absorption by a few families of the people's wealth," spread universal education, and establish economic security for all. Later, in a Thanksgiving sermon celebrating, ironically

enough, the election of Ulysses S. Grant to the presidency, Haven urged
Methodists to make their lives an offering by which to speed the achievement of social equality, racial intermarriage, woman's suffrage, temper-
ance reform, and other beauties of the millennium.[34]

But then, strangely enough, the next fifty years of Protestant
church history in America were to see two contradictory tendencies
develop. On the one hand, the god of "Yankee arms" went marching
on. In 1864, evangelicals launched a National Reform Association
that aspired

> to maintain existing Christian features in the American government, and
> to secure such an amendment to the Constitution of the United States
> as will indicate that this is a Christian nation, and will place all the
> Christian laws, institutions and usages of our government on an undeni-
> able legal basis in the fundamental law of the land.[35]

The corruption in this hope for a "Christian America" was not far
from the old medieval dream of a Holy Roman Empire. As historian
Robert T. Handy puts it for Protestants in the early nineteenth
century:

> The priority of the religious vision was strongly and widely maintained;
> it was Christianity *and* civilization, Christianity as the best part of civili-
> zation, and its hope. In the latter part of the century, however, in most
> cases unconsciously, much of the real focus had shifted to the civilization
> itself, with Christianity and the churches finding their significance in
> relation to it.[36]

The corruption here was double. The idea of a "Christian America"
tended to blind many Protestants to the rank, unbiblical exploitations
of certain Americans—the Indian, the urban factory workers, the
newly freed and resegregated black. Also the very content of Biblically rooted Christianity came easily to be confused with the content
of the United States Constitution. That church history began, not
with Protestant America, but with the death and resurrection of the
Lord of lords, could easily be forgotten by promoters of this Ameri-
canist social gospel.

But a parallel corruption among some post-Civil War evangelicals
was equally momentous. In the backwash of great wars, religion in

America seems to suffer demonstrable setbacks. Not only did the Civil War seem to bring an illusory "settlement" of the great moral question of slavery in America, but it released in victors and vanquished alike new passions for wealth and power that took shape in railroads, factories, immigrations, commerce, and imperious nationalism. Among some of the revival leaders of the prewar era, such aftermaths of the war were not to be celebrated. Industrial America was not the Kingdom of God. In a dogged attempt to distinguish the two, they turned to preaching a gospel of deliverance from an evil world.[37] The *ethic* associated with this deliverance concentrated on personal purity, "understood increasingly as 'no smoking, no drinking, no dancing, and no gambling'—the elements that came to characterize the revivalistic ethic" of the early twentieth century.[38] No one had to be a learned student of the New Testament to know that these elements were hardly what Jesus meant by "the weightier demands of the Law" (Matt. 23:23). Nor were they the weightier matters of contemporary American history from the Civil War of the 1860's to the Great Depression of the 1930's.

Was Protestantism of this era demonstrating its inability to conceive, practice, and organize a version of the Christian life that was at once personal and social, historically reflective and contemporarily perceptive, critical of evil in the world and repentant for the church's implication in that evil? The question began to ring out in late-nineteenth-century America. It echoes, with strange pertinence, in American ears listening today. Josiah Strong, surveying the national Protestant scene in 1913, was touching reality when he described the "two-party system" of the twentieth-century American churches. One, he said, was "individualistic," the other "social." Extending Strong's analysis, Martin Marty put it as follows:

One party, which may be called "Private" Protestantism, seized that name "evangelical" which had characterized all Protestants early in the nineteenth century. It accented individual salvation out of the world, personal moral life congruent with the ideals of the saved, and fulfillment or its absence in the rewards or punishments in another world in a life to come. The second informal group, which can be called "Public" Protestantism, was public insofar as it was more exposed to the social order and the social destinies of men.[39]

The link between a deeply personal and a broadly social experience of religious faith seems to have been broken among American Protestants in the late nineteenth century. It remained unrestored in the twentieth. The break became glaring in the 1920's. By then the social energies of Protestantism seemed exhausted over Prohibition. The Modernist-Fundamentalist theological controversy built up steam inside the churches while society outside was "roaring" toward the disaster of 1929.[40] Beset by the pessimisms of the 1920–1950 era, "neo-orthodox" theologians arose to tame the pretensions of "moral men" who seek too easily to solve the problems of an "immoral society."[41] But even these brilliant critics of three hundred years of Protestant hopes for a continent-wide "city upon a hill" lived out their lives in the midst of the two-party Protestantism which many readers recognize as familiar in their own upbringing.

Looking back over the whole of the long history of the Christian church, one of those neo-orthodox theologians, H. Richard Niebuhr, summarized much of this very history from a standpoint peculiarly relevant to the American portion of the history, as he wrote in 1935:

> A converted church in a corrupt civilization withdraws to its upper rooms, into monasteries and conventicles; it issues forth from these in the aggressive evangelism of apostles, monks, and friars, circuit riders and missionaries; it relaxes its rigorism as it discerns signs of repentance and faith; it enters into inevitable alliance with converted emperors and governors, philosophers and artists, merchants and entrepreneurs, and begins to live at peace in the culture they produce under the stimulus of their faith; when faith loses its force, as generation follows generation, discipline is relaxed, repentance grows formal, corruption enters with idolatry, and the church, tied to the culture which it sponsored, suffers corruption with it. Only a new withdrawal followed by a new aggression can then save the church and restore to it the salt with which to savor society.[42]

HOPES AND FEARS AGAIN

Can the churches be the salt to savor American society in the late twentieth century? With what "new withdrawal and new aggression"? Can we recover, uncover, or discover a form of faith and life adequate to the worship of the God of the Hebrews and Christians, and their search for a just and merciful society? The question is as old as Abraham, Jeremiah, and Jesus. It is as young as the debate, in a 1976 American Presidential campaign, over the significance of personal Christian faith for the political leadership of a nation celebrating its bicentennial.

We began this book with such questions. We have tried to deepen the questions through three chapters of Biblical and historical recollection. We continue now, seeking answers on that always perilous frontier between the present and the future, crossable on bridges built from those compounds of facts, hopes, and fears by which humans shape their history. Our further exploration will take us not only into more realms of historical analysis and theological argument but also into *looking* at the world in which all of us now live. To have looked, in Christian faith, at the world of the past presupposes something reassuring about the world of the present. It, too, will be worth looking at by some future generation of human beings, in their own future century.

If they are Christians, what will our descendants see to value in this time of the church's history in America? What would we want them to see and value? With those very questions, the rest of these pages will be intimately concerned.

Chapter 5

American City Dwellers

Four chapters ago we began with a glimpse into the life crises of six persons living in six different urban areas of the United States. We were told nothing about the religious beliefs or church-synagogue relationships of these people. Three of them are actual people, and three are "imaginary" in the sense that the authors know people *like* them.

Shirley Weatherford (by another name) lives in Atlanta, thanks to the services of that county emergency squad. She happens to be a member of a suburban Presbyterian church, but her recent life-and-near-death history connects her most vividly with Louella McCabe of Boston. What these two women have in common is a medical problem that needed solving at a particular time: the one, when she suffered a heart attack; the other, when she became pregnant with her son Tommy. What they have by contrast is their degree of *access* to local urban medical services. We have come a long way since those days of St. Francis, when the starving, sick, demoralized urban poor lifted grateful hands for the simple ministrations of the wandering friar. Jostled by medical science, on the one side, and the growth of wealth on the other, American city dwellers have come to expect doctors and hospitals as part of their environment. If your name is Shirley Weatherford, your expectations along this line have recently been heightened. You know, in the most personal way, how dependent your very life can be on the instant availability of the practical medical knowledge of how to save victims of an attack of heart fibrillation. If your name is Louella McCabe, you have much vaguer, even more cynical expectations. In fact, when you get the hospital's medical report on your son Tommy next month and you see the final diagnostic note in the report—"probably due to prenatal or early natal malnourishment"—you sink into your chair overwhelmed by a sense of bitterness and despair. There was a time when your baby boy might have been helped to grow up as a normal child. That time is past, forever.

We can well imagine further differences in the way that these two women perceive their life worlds. If each has faith in God, what does that faith cause them to do? The one, we suspect, spent some hours of worship in her church enormously *thankful* for the neighborly care which her community managed to give her in a desperate hour. The other may well have things in her life for which she can be thankful to God; but, as for the physically impaired mind of her five-year-old son, she has nothing but the suffering of the oppressed to form into a prayer. The form of the oppression differs, but her feelings as a black resident of Roxbury make her a kinswoman of that ancient brickmaker in Egypt, with whom we early had our imaginary interview. If Mrs. McCabe attends a church in Roxbury, its minister probably knows how to preach with moving power about the deliverance of the Children of Israel from Egypt. But deliverance of her son from a numbed, malnourished mind eludes her. Ironically, she lives in the city whose Puritan founders hoped to make it a model city— a "city upon a hill."

Harrisene Little and Philip Delaney live literally and figuratively on opposite coasts of American society; but, in a haunting way, they grew up sharing a vision of their social future that remains within hailing distance of Boston's Puritan fathers and mothers. Each came early to believe in the importance of the country's formal educational system; each nourished ambition for self and children as "productive citizens" in both a country and a world. Neither, in short, showed any early signs of deep alienation from the community of people called Americans. Each participated through their family in the pain of the Vietnam war of the '60s. We do not know how her own children respond to the American dream, but we do know that Mrs. Little affirms the "up from poverty" element of the Protestant ethic —not only for herself but for her ghetto neighbors as well. She wants to spend her life helping them to overcome the burdens of poverty that, by some miracle, failed to cripple her.

In his own wide-angled way, Delaney harbors the same hope. He likes to see his work at the bank as a ministry of upbuilding for poor people in places like Hong Kong, Seoul, and Tokyo. One suspects that his devotion to systems of benefit for the world's poor is no sham for him. His children have caught something of that vision from him and rather turned it against him. His son has seen the evil in a war that imposed American power and values upon a local Asian society struggling against poverty in a context quite different from that of the American pioneer. His daughter has widened her net of compassion to encompass the ailing, impoverished sectors of her California natural environment. And Philip apparently agrees so deeply with his children's appropriation of his own dream that he has deep reservations now about the system. San Francisco, one of the great "alabaster cities" of America, now has some of its gleam rubbed off. He might not even entertain these reservations, or be able to react so soberly to the opinions of his children, if he did not have—along with Harrisene Little—a continuing array of hopes and fears that comprise a sort of religion. Like Tarrou and Rieux in *The Plague,* does he have his own inward "bay" in which he sometimes swims on the perimeters of his city, catching a glimpse, perhaps, of a better city "beyond the years" of the 1970's?[1] We cannot be sure. But one suspects that Philip Delaney is at a critical juncture in his life. Aged fifty, he must either rediscover the dream of his youth or revise it for service to the last decades of his life. He is a good example of an American who stands on that perilous frontier between the present and the future of human history.

On the surface, neither Paul Ransom nor Luis Fernández has much in common with each other or the other four. They are citizens of two different countries. As a bureaucrat in one, Paul has no official jurisdiction over the affairs of the other. He is subject to laws that restrict his ability to give attention to the troubles of the Fernández family ninety miles from Mexico City. Yet, Luis is another figurative-literal illustration of the hopes and fears of Americans north and south of the equator. He lives on the boundary of United States society. He wants to get into that society for the classic reason of adding a bit to his wealth. At least for a few days he thus joined a group in our national society to whom Paul's governmental Department of Health, Education, and Welfare has at least temporary obligations. Ransom knows that Luis Fernández represents one little personal ripple in the sea-sized world hunger problem. That problem laps about the borders of the United States, swirling with the rage, envy, and despair of earth's two thirds of poor people. In his own bureaucratic nightmares, Ransom has despairs of his own. What if even inside the United States we are unable to organize society so that our own hungry get food, and our own sick get to the hospital in time? Can we help our own poorly informed citizens secure the keys for unlocking a livable human tomorrow? Right now Ransom sees himself as part of a bureaucratic system enveloped in a haze. It has insufficient communication with its various publics, an insufficiency, he says, which is "the deliberate creation of an organization that does not want to reveal itself too clearly lest it lose some of its prerogatives. In my dream the maze represented all that cluster of delays, dodges, buckpassing, paper-shuffling, ego-building, turf-defining, and evaluations that are typical of my bureaucracy. No wonder one cannot count on a given turnstile or a given alley. The 'system' works on its own behalf."[2]

One can well imagine how Jeremiah might respond to Ransom's dream analysis: "Government bureaucrats can be as idolatrous as Jerusalem temple worshipers!" And the apostle Paul: "The Roman and the American empires are not all that different!" Augustine: "The love of power and money can ruin the love of God and the love of human beings!" Calvin: "The reformation of the human city toward justice and mercy never ends!" John Winthrop: "We have forgotten to seek our neighbor's good in pursuit of our own!" And Charles Finney: "Our hearts and our associations need redemption!" Paul Ransom will not necessarily hear these echoes from prophets of the past who have dreamed of a "Godly order" in human affairs. But inside his nightmare, presupposed by it, is its mirror opposite: a vision of an international society in which persons will not have to trek over the border for their survival; of a national society in which Tommy McCabe will not be born hungry; of a local society in which Harrisene Little really gets the job she seeks—and so on to the life story of every person imaginable who has ever read the eleventh chapter of Hebrews and who has understood "such a man" as Thomas Wolfe, who wrote about his own coming to New York City in this lyrical prose:

When such a man . . . comes first to the great city—but how can we speak of such a man coming first to the great city, when really the great city is within him, encysted in his heart, built up in all the flaming images of his brain: a symbol of his hope, the image of his high desire, the final crown, the citadel of all that he has ever dreamed of or longed for or imagined that life could bring to him? For such a man as this, there really is no coming to the city. He brings the city with him everywhere he goes, and when that final moment comes when he at last breathes in the city's air, feels his foot upon the city street, looks around him at the city's pinnacles, into the dark, unceasing tide of city faces, grips his sinews, feels his flesh, pinches himself to make sure he is really there—for such a man as this, and for such a moment, it will always be a question to be considered in its bewildering ramifications by the subtle soul psychologists to know which city is the real one, which city he has found and seen, which city for this man is really there.[3]

FACT, VALUE, AND SOCIAL SCIENCE

What sort of kingdom—or political community—might we be capable of building as living American citizens? This is the burden of the rest of our inquiry. We want to enrich the inquiry here with some findings from social science.

Science contributes to the "collision of dreams" in the modern world. The collision occurs around a subject rather new in human affairs: the fact-value conflict. For centuries a certain tribe of Australian aborigines conceived their life patterns as rooted in an ancient "dreamtime." Life for them means circling out from, and back into, the great original Dream of the gods and the forebears.[4] We have said that the Hebrews' faith in their Lord compelled them to "straighten out" the circle of history, to make it a line, to conceive their lives together as a pilgrimage. One legacy of this view, in our own century, is that most people think of the future as about to be different from the past. Aided by the concept of evolution, we think "historically." We see the present as "explained" in large measure by the past, and the future as somehow rooted in the present. We say "somehow," because the *way* that a dead-and-done past *becomes* a still-to-be-born future remains quite mysterious. After all, many elements in human history have remained constant over a million years.

The human physique is an example. Other elements have changed rapidly in our own lifetimes—e.g., the speed of travel and communication. But there is the mystery: What accounts for the balance, the different paces, and the various mixes of continuity and change in human affairs?

A view that answers, "random chance," satisfies some thinkers, such as genetic biologists. A view that answers, "strict determination of one fact by other facts," satisfies others, such as disciples of the psychologist B. F. Skinner. But neither of these views grapples deeply enough with the mystery of continuity and change in human *societies.* Why did Greek rule yield to Roman? Roman religion to Christian? the Catholic law against usury to the Protestant toleration of interest? the settled life of the New England Puritan to the unsettled life of the American frontier? No reflective account of any of these movements of human history will conclude that they occurred either by mere chance or by rigid predetermination. Not even the Bible, which introduces us to a divine power able to defeat Egyptian armies and to overrule Roman executioners, treats human history either as a dice throw or as the start-up of a machine. *Between* the "given facts" of the past and the still unreal "facts" of the future, something intervenes. It is neither bare fact nor bare fancy. What shall we call this mysterious intervention?

Social scientists have sometimes called it "human values." So far we have used the term sparingly, because modern philosophy makes it an eye of an intellectual hurricane that has rocked Western culture for at least three centuries. In modern culture we sense the difference between "facts" and "values" almost as unconsciously as we sense the difference between rocks and clouds. Indeed, modern culture gives us a rocky feeling about fact, and a cloudy feeling about value. The one is just there, solid, indisputable. The other is misty, subject to evaporation, always in danger of not being there. Facts "speak for themselves"; values speak with a whisper. Our very ears and brain cells are predisposed to hear the signal "important!" parading like a trumpet before fact; the signal "unreal" dogs the trail of everything called value.

What we have written in Chapters 1–4 breaks with this whole description of the-way-things-are and the-way-things-change. Our aphorism, *The past we celebrate pre-enacts the future we hope for,* obviously collides with a dualistic, fact-value description of *human* history and culture. Australian aborigines are so certain their dream-time is *real* that they perpetually shape their action around that reality to make it current, alive, and powerful for the future. The faithful Jew remembers Moses in the midst of Treblinka and revolts against the Nazi, thus making a new bit of history. The faithful Christian remembers Jesus the risen Lord, and is prepared to over-throw the religious pretensions of empire. The Puritan dreams of a city founded on true faith and ethics, and migrates to New England. An orphaned girl in The Bronx dreams of a college education and begins to get one at the age of twenty-six. A frustrated bureaucrat dreams of justice for the oppressed through a reformed bureaucratic system, and (who knows?) by 1980 malnutrition in Roxbury declines drastically. From this view of human history, *values are factual too.* And facts are valuable, some more than others! But to use the words "facts" and "values" in this context so obscures the context itself that we prefer to use the words as little as possible opposite each other.

We are about to report about an inquiry into the network of feelings, ideas, interpersonal and institutional relationships of a group of urban citizens in a certain part of the United States. We want to report some valuable facts about these people, and some values which these people seem to embrace and to enact factually in their life relationships. To slice any of this into parcels marked "facts" and "values" remains impossible for countless human beings in their ordinary day-to-day existence. In short: to take "history" seriously, to write it, and to make it requires just this refusal of every such split in the description or the performance of the human drama. As the late Kenneth Underwood put it: "What one knows about the world, and what one plans to do in it, are in constant and creative relation-ship."[5] To say it another way: "The highest test of a civilization is its sense of fact."[6]

Another way to explore this momentous intellectual issue is to ask whether "social research" has any value to people in our time. Cer-tainly many religious people doubt that it has. What difference should it make that church attendance among Catholics under thirty declined from 55 percent to 41 percent from 1966 to 1974?[7] Just another random fact unrelated to anything really important. But, on sober reflection, neither the Jewish nor the Christian religions encourage that cavalier attitude toward human social facts. As the preceding chapters attest, students of the Biblical faith take "history" seriously. They do so because they believe that human history has in it, concretely and visibly, the Lord of All Being. Jews and Christians believe in anything but an "unworldly" God. What happens in this world makes a difference to him; he means it to make a difference to us. Information about one's human neighbors one may receive in a spirit of cool detachment. A cry of "Fire!" does not *have* to move anybody to leave the television set for the street. But as this illustration suggests, most of the information that comes to us from our neighbors is already set in some interpretive framework; some set of signals enable us to say, "This fact is trivial," or "This fact is important."

Every social research project enters the minds of the researchers via the signals, the lenses, the windows of just such a framework. In our own two cases, our participation in the Urban Policy Study had long preparation in our study of the Biblical-historical perspectives and our experience of residence in the cities about to be described. This background helped surface for us a question that sounds naive and nonsensical to many a secular ear: *Who are the People of God in modern urban society?* Several of our colleagues were not professing Christians or Jews, so this language does not happen to be theirs. One blank in the question would probably revise it sufficiently for them: "Who are the people of _____ in modern urban society?" One colleague might have filled in the blank with a phrase like, "broadest and most accurate understanding"; another would have said, "most political effectiveness"; and another might have preferred, "responsibility." One and all, we wanted to learn something about the conditions, the relationships, the circumstances associated with defining and *enhancing the best qualities of human life* in the American urban community. Of no member in our research team could it be said that he or she was "value-neutral."[8]

In virtually every word of the undisputed portion of our question, some preference peeks out. Take "modern urban society," for example. Social scientists are interested in "society," a portion of reality that does not much include what astronomers study. Within their own "universe of discourse," however, social scientists do ask universal questions, such as, What is the division of opinion on this issue among *all* persons in a certain society? By taking that question seriously social scientists have laboriously developed the sampling technique familiar to us all now in the form of political polls. To begin our search for information on 400,000 residents of our urban area, for example, we chose to interview approximately one in every 450 persons of the area—about 900 in all. The aim in drawing this sample was to find a "miniature version" of the whole urban area including every major similarity and difference between the population: age, sex, race, residential location, and the like. The care with which this sample was assembled embodied one of the profound ethical dimensions of the best social science: the principle that no person should be unrepresented in any generalization the scientist makes about "society." Without doubt, this principle can never be perfectly followed; but the discipline of attempting such universality penetrates social science with a version of *justice* which deserves admiration from the viewpoint of the Hebrew-Christian ethic.

Like everything else human, research is selective in its object of study. We selected a *local* urban society as object of our focus. But we did so in the expectation and with the inward obligation of searching for the connection between *this* local urban society and others in the world. Even here, the rule of all-possible-universality bore down upon us, again expressing a sort of justice that seeks to protect human projects from provincialism. There is one provincialism inherent in much modern social research, especially that heavily dependent upon "surveys"; and that is, provincialism in *time*. Historians criticize modern polltakers for their preoccupation with the modern. History, they say, is a movie that tells about the dynamic movement of human affairs over stretches of time. Social science, they say, is just still photography, just the retouching of single frames of celluloid. The result is chronological snobbery that overestimates the worth of *now*.

The social scientist's reply here can be both firm and modest: firm, in the belief that, as the quality of a movie relates to the quality of individual frames, so every moment of human history is worth study-

ing carefully; modest, in confessing, with Max Weber, that "every scientific 'fulfillment' . . . asks to be surpassed and outdated."[9] Here, one has almost to speak of the "faith" of scientists of all sorts: that, however surpassed and outdated, their discoveries will fit into some purpose, some value, some meaning in the human enterprise as a whole. Is that utterly removed from the faith of a Jeremiah? Though they would not all agree with the optimistic Browning that "there never was one lost good," social scientists seem to ask questions of their contemporaries in the hope that truth rightly learned about one moment in history will have its place of value for other, future moments. Without an implicit hope like that, none of us gets up in the morning with enthusiasm.

A Developing City

Our city is really an urbanizing area containing three small cities —Raleigh, Durham, and Chapel Hill. Our state—North Carolina— is one of the least urbanized in the country, having only one city (Charlotte) with a population as large as 300,000. Our region—the southeast—might be similarly described: the last to experience economic growth associated with urban industrial capitalism; the last to become a part of "modern America"—the last, partly because it tried, through a disastrous war, to secede politically from nineteenth-century America.

Why concentrate a considerable portion of this study now upon research findings on this lesser-known urban region? A prompt, inadequate, but necessary preliminary answer is theological. From the perspective of Christians who learned to follow the "good that came out of Nazareth" (John 1:46) there are no uninteresting, unimportant human places anymore. From this perspective, Plains, Georgia, did not need Jimmy Carter to make it interesting. Such a conviction, we think, carries over into one of the most general, most crucial presuppositions of modern science: all empirical reality is worth investigating.[10]

But our reasons for reporting our investigations of Raleigh, Durham, and Chapel Hill, North Carolina, are more numerous. First, these cities are no small part of our personal histories. One of us lives here as we complete this book (1977), and the other spent ten years (1962–1972) living here. For better or worse, our understanding of ourselves, our urban neighbors, and the promise of American urban life has been pervasively shaped by our experience of citizenship in this particular place.

A second, less personal range of reasons for our geographical focus relates to the history of American religion sketched in Chapter 4. The elements central to that sketch have a certain high visibility in central North Carolina, a visibility that makes the region especially interesting from this historical point of view. The Second Great Awakening swept through this area, then largely rural, in the nineteenth century. The revivals left their imprint upon the culture of the region, laying the ground for the growth of large Baptist, Methodist, Presbyterian, and other Low Church constituencies that still dominate the area. Muffled by the devastations of war and an outdated agricultural system, the spirit of capitalism began finally to penetrate the region in the late nineteenth century through such events as the rise of tobacco manufacturing in Durham. Simultaneously, state and local leaders of the area did their part in building the New South through educational institutions. Three large universities and several smaller ones stand in these three cities, among them the University of North Carolina, Duke University, North Carolina State University, and North Carolina Central University. Currently enrolling over 50,000 students, these and other schools form the basis for the region's emerging major industry: the production of knowledge.

This latter characteristic of the region fits closely with a third reason for our interest in it: For about a century two of the universities have lived in close relationship to another dimension of its history: state politics. The state capital is located here, and "political policy" might be said to be the second major locally manufactured product. Education for the professions of law, business, medicine, and teaching has long been centered—for the entire state—in the university at Chapel Hill. Since the 1880's education and research in the sciences and technologies at the university in Raleigh has sent several generations of technically trained persons to the farms, industries, governments, and other institutions of the state. The region thus happens to be one of the places in the United States where several powerful ingredients of modern society (and modern city-building) are present in obvious ways: a cultural commitment to economic growth, the technical tools of science, and the decision-making tools of political institutions. An important local embodiment of these three ingredients is a highly successful enterprise called the Research Triangle Park. It is a joint creation of industry, the major local universities, and the state government. Over seventy-five laboratories, research institutes, factories, and governmental bureaus currently inhabit the Park. Activity there ranges from the manufacture of communications equipment by the world's largest computer producer, to research on textile fibers by a major chemical company, to research on air and water pollution by the U.S. Government's Environmental Protection Agency, to the investigation of world population problems by an interuniversity institute.

Like people in many other of the newer urban centers of the United States and around the world, citizens of this region have a growing number of reasons to think of themselves as part of the "modern world." They live in a part of the United States which for long—economically speaking, at least—has had much in common with developing countries. In blunt "progress" language, that has often meant wearing the badge of "backward." Nothing seems more characteristic of the world of 1977 than the refusal of growing numbers of people the world around to wear that badge. In this respect, the 400,000 persons living in this urbanizing, three-county area of central North Carolina have much reason to think of themselves as participants in the modern world.

A final major reason for our study relates to the historic two-party issue—personal versus social religion—among American churches past and present. Our concern for this issue has been deeply colored by a mixture of our experience as professionals in our work and our emerging beliefs as participants in local church life. As a psychotherapist one of us over the years has entered into probing conversation with hundreds of persons about their individual problems. For many of these persons, no understanding or solution to their problems seems to be possible apart from their learning new ways of relating to (1) other people and (2) basic life meanings which have the quality of religion as defined in the first chapter of this book. Often the lack of satisfying personal meaning and interpersonal relationships comes to a crisis with these folk in their work for some institution. Both in our work and in our life as citizens, we too have experienced the frustrations of a poor "fit" between the persons, the organizations, and the preferred meanings of our lives. Most of the reasons that challenge *us* to get out of bed in the morning with enthusiasm relate to these diverse relationships to other people. Our own experience, therefore, assaults us with great puzzlement concerning such claims as, "Religion and politics don't mix," or "What one believes is his or her own business." Such an "ethical theory" lacks resonance in our experience. The historic split between "private" and "public" religion among United States church people haunts us with the same sense of unreality. In a book published recently one of us came down to this way of describing the unreality:

> Often [in American churches] . . . for lack of coherent perceptions of scientific-historical fact in some ideological-religious perspective, the symbolic proclamations of the churches have sounded hollow and unworldly. The "two-world" theory of religion and society is one possible theory; but crisis—personal and social—is hard on that theory in human terms. Sober reflection on everyday life is equally hard on it: human beings seem not to live by religion alone, ideology, money, votes, or bread alone. In fact they live by all of these things in some sort of wholeness. Out of their belief in the possibility of such wholeness, the institutions of religion presumably justify their continued existence.[11]

The Biblical faith by which both of us want to live affirms "the possibility of such wholeness" for human beings. But contemporary American life compels us to perceive the difficulties that many Americans, ourselves included, have in doing so. The difficulties seem to accumulate amid the very developments that mark the Raleigh–Durham–Chapel Hill region as "urban" and "modern": mechanization, mass production, and affluence in the economy; increasing dependence of individuals upon others for the meeting of even simple human needs; the increasing role of government in everyday affairs; the power of knowledge and technology to reshape everyday environment; mobility and change in one's neighbors, friends, ideas, and images; and a growing sense that one's personal life cannot escape the intrusions of such complex events as one's dependence upon a car to get to work with gas whose price escalates at the whim of producers thousands of miles around the globe. In a society like this, *how* does one "get it all together"? Or, in another more classical cliché, how does one "get religion"? The answer has often slumbered and sometimes shouted in our lives: No human being gets it all together all by himself or herself.

With whose help, under what circumstances, in what patterns of interhuman relationship do modern urban people achieve personal-social wholeness? This is an empirical question, growing out of a certain philosophical slant on American history. In all of its ramifications, the question led us in 1971, along with a group of academic and civic colleagues, to devise a social research program which we called the Urban Policy Study. One hunch behind the study was that a fair number of citizens in our urban area had beliefs, perceptions, and experiences which contradict the assertion that personal life is one thing, social relationships another. Another hunch was that the facts about this contradiction have their roots in historical developments of economics, politics, and religion in America. And yet another was that the divorce of the personal and the social in all these realms of American life is due for momentous revision, not only in terms of what ought to happen but in terms of what already is happening to people who live in cities like Raleigh, Durham, and Chapel Hill. What we did to test these hunches we would like now to narrate.

SEARCHING FOR THE PEOPLE OF GOD

Christians we may be, but the two authors are not so uninstructed that we would go looking for the People of God in our city simply by visiting places called churches. Nothing in our impressions of Jeremiah, Jesus, or Paul suggests that they expected their followers to become visible in human society only in their church attendance. We have seen in the New Testament that the people called Christians had certain marks of their faith in their inward life as a fellowship and in their outward witness to the world. Though some dimensions of their life were hard to understand or even recognize from a distance, most of the marks were publicly ascertainable. We remember that they: (1) trusted the God and Father of Jesus Christ enough to worship him publicly, sometimes at risk of their lives; (2) encouraged one another to "keep the faith" and to share it with people outside the church in an active way; (3) welcomed a wide variety of "strangers" into their fellowship and did good to strangers who needed help, whether or not they joined the fellowship; (4) and in other ways practiced an ethic of upbuilding of their neighbor, even at the cost of some pleasure and good to themselves.[12] Anyone can see both continuity and discontinuity between those characteristics of the first-century Christians and the church of the following centuries. We have every occasion, therefore, to ask about the presence or absence of such a people in other times and places. Would the tools of social science give us any help in our own time for locating people who share characteristics like the above four? Or in determining the fact of their absence? Our Urban Policy Study was one attempt to find out.

The four characteristics, we suggested to ourselves, could be translated into the more secular language of four clusters of specific questions to 900 people in our urban sample. Each cluster would seek information about these four dimensions of the citizen's personal-social existence. (We have listed below only a few of the many questions actually used for this part of the survey.)

1. In general do you see yourself as surrounded by circumstances and people worthy of your *trust?*
   "Would you say that most people can be trusted or that you have to be very careful in dealing with people?"
   "Would you say that most of the time people try to be helpful or that they are mostly just looking out for themselves?"
   "Are you sure that some of the friends you have will never turn their backs on you?"

2. Do you tend to *act* on what you *believe?*
   "If you knew that a certain street crossing was dangerous for schoolchildren, would you do something about it?"
   "When it comes to a problem like crime in this community, do people like yourself have some ability to do something about it?"

3. Do you welcome relationships with *all human beings,* regardless of race, sex, or social status?

"Do you see one race as better than other races?"

"Should there be a law against intermarriage between members of different races?"

"How strongly would you object if a member of your family wanted to bring a black (white) friend home to dinner?"

"Would you say that most black (white) people can be trusted or that you have to be very careful in dealing with black (white) people?"

"Who should have the final say in major family decisions: the man, the woman, or both?"

"Who makes better decisions: men or women, or does it depend on the individual?"

4. Do you tend to have enough *regard for public need* to move you on occasion to sacrifice some good of your own for public good?

"Should a person sometimes give up time with the family in order to work for good government?"

"Should a person be willing to risk losing some friendships for the sake of good government?"

"Which is more important to you—to work for a pay raise in one's job or to work for good government?"

Much more elaborately than this summary would suggest, our interviewers asked our sample of citizens for many details about their life situations. Like most social scientists we were interested to know the relation of their answers to questions like the above to their age, race, sex, education, income, etc. A relatively small number balked at such inquiry, even though the interview ran on, in some cases, two or three hours. When you think about it, the patience that many Americans show to wandering sociological interviews is amazing. Why put up with so many apparently nosy questions? Our assurances of anonymity do not seem enough to explain it. Rather, we believe that people answer survey questions eagerly when they perceive that their opinion is somehow being taken seriously. The lonely people in our sample sometimes prolonged the interview beyond the interviewer's patience. After all, what is more complimentary than the readiness of a fellow human being to treat your knowledge, your opinion, your life as important? Many in our society hunger for that compliment. When done with an honest intention to serve a community's welfare with the findings, survey research can thus be morally significant even in its procedures.

How did responses to these four categories of questions vary in connection with the church membership of the respondents? Given that the four traits (let us tag them as Trust, Action Potential, Racial Openness, and Public Regard) are associated with Judeo-Christian heritage, it is reasonable to look at involvement in synagogues and churches as a condition favoring the occurrence of these traits in people. Our urban area is well known for its large Protestant church membership. At the same time, as a rapidly growing area with much in-migration, the region becomes more pluralistic by the year. The high concentration of sophisticated industry, universities, and technical research facilities in the area ensure more cultural diversity than outsiders assume of the so-called Bible Belt. For statistical comparisons at least, there were quite enough persons in our sample of 900 to claim "no religious affiliation" or "no active church membership" to permit us to construct a meaningful comparative Level of Religious Involvement Scale for all respondents. Our question probed the respondent's patterns of church attendance, church membership, and leadership in the church. We added up the answers on these matters and were able to divide our 900 persons into four levels of comparative involvement in churches or synagogues. We then looked at all the scores on the traits of Trust, Action Potential, Racial Openness, and Public Regard. Did persons with a high Religious Involvement also score highly on these four traits? Our initial finding will disappoint those who espouse church traditions. The relationship to Action Potential, Public Regard, and Trust is not noticeably different for church attenders compared to nonattenders. The relationship of religious involvement to Racial Openness is in the "wrong" direction. That is, people who are members of churches are *more* likely to be prejudiced racially than agnostics or atheists![13]

Unfortunately for this and other social scientific studies, however, such findings represent a rather superficial "pass" at the question. So far in our own inquiry, for example, we have no information on the effect of the distinction that seemed to grow so sharply in American churches in the late nineteenth century: the distinction between "public" and "private" religion. If a certain respondent is "highly involved" in a local church whose leaders have long ignored, inside the church, such "political issues" as the citizen's obligation to vote, there is nothing surprising about the lack of correlation between church involvement and public Action Potential. Furthermore, given the typically segregated pattern of church organizations in this country, one can imagine a number of reasons why church membership might confirm racial prejudice more often than undermine it. At the very least, what this level of the inquiry sustains is the theological observation of prophets like Jeremiah: attendance at churchly worship services is not *by itself* an ethical mark of membership in the People of God.

Suppose, however, that it makes a great difference whether one joins a local congregation wholly committed to private religion or one committed to public religion as well. For purposes of answering this question, we developed an Ethical-Religious Scale. The idea here was not to test for "right" or "wrong" views of specific social issues such as civil rights laws or tax reform or equal rights for women, but merely to see how persons differed significantly in the four traits if they also differed in their answers to such questions as:

"Are public issues discussed at your church?"
"If a church has only enough money either to build a new sanctuary or to help some people with social problems, which should it be?"

The results proved interesting. We found a substantial relationship between the discussion of issues in a religious context and Racial Openness. The relationship to Action Potential was also mildly encouraging. *Apparently the Judeo-Christian tradition of justice and mercy has some impact on social attitudes if issues are deliberated within the context of congregational life.* The relationships to Trust and Public Regard were positive but relatively weak. This suggests that even this subpopulation of churchgoers, who bring their social concerns to the church, are frequently lacking both in interpersonal affirmation and in willingness to be concerned for those beyond their immediate circle if some cost is involved. By contrast with the vivid images of social justice and social compassion that dominate the prophetic and the apostolic literature of the Bible, their scores on Action Potential and Racial Openness still fall short of what one might expect of "the salt of the earth."

One gets a picture here of a subgroup of ethically concerned church people who have made real headway against racial prejudice in themselves and who see political activity as an outworking of their religious faith. But at the same time they seem to lack trust in people around them, and they call a halt to political activity that demands much self-sacrifice. When translated into pictures of particular human beings, the result is troubling. However she acquired it, Harrisene Little needed an amazingly deep level of trust in officials of the school system, for example, for her pursuit of an education. Without a very large "public regard" she would have hardly nourished an ambition to return as a professional to the very ghetto out of which she emerged as a child. So recently restored to health by a kind of urban-technological miracle, Shirley Weatherford will need a network of trustworthy fellow citizens and a similarly high regard for the public if she is to use her recovery from that heart attack as an occasion to do something about a possibly grim answer to a question like: "How many of Georgia's 159 counties have a medical rescue unit like my county's?" Philip Delaney started his career with a high level of Public Regard, all right; but in recent years his trust level has plummeted. He is no longer sure that he has a set of business colleagues who can be counted on to work with him in realizing his dreams of international peace and justice. So also with the church people in our Urban Policy Study: *people with high Ethical-Religious scores often give empirical evidence of lacking both interpersonal affirmation and willingness to be concerned for those beyond their immediate circle if some cost is involved.*

What we have been doing here resembles the classic search for a needle in a haystack. Only we have no way of being sure that in this haystack there exists any needle at all. The theological side of our intelligence inclines toward the conviction, "Of course a group of people with the marks of the People of God can be found in our community." But the convictions of theology become the hypotheses of social science, which moves by the simple, devastating rule: "Let's see." So, doggedly and hopefully, we made a third pass at our stack of data, adding to the analytical tools one further dimension. Building on the notion, evident in the careers of religious leaders from Jeremiah to Augustine to Charles G. Finney, that the Biblical faith calls its exponents to life in "two cities," we asked ourselves and our data: *Is the Biblical ethic to be found in its greatest vitality among people who exhibit alternating involvements in a small community and in the larger public?* To answer this question we constructed a Citizen Involvement Scale concerning such public activities as campaigning for candidates for office; signing petitions; attending conventions; and participating in voluntary groups acting on such issues as community race relations, environmental responsibility, and the world population and hunger problems. So far as we know, the empirical hypothesis here is unique in the history of the investigations of religion in twentieth-century American life: *Will a subsample of citizens, high on both Ethical-Religious Participation and Citizen Involvement, score markedly higher than other groups on our four marks of the People of God—Trust, Action Potential, Racial Openness, and Public Regard?*

The results were startling! Though statistics sometimes look boring, the graphs on pp. 110–111, we believe, are alive with meaning for the partisans of both public and private religion in the United States of America. Numbers can lie. We believe that these numbers tell some exciting truth.

The graphs here show the scores on only two of the four marks —Action Potential and Racial Openness. The findings with the other two—Trust and Public Regard—are similar: The chances that any person will score *high* on any mark *increases* with (1) increasing political involvement, (2) increasing participation in a church that affirms public religion, and (3) increasingly satisfying relations with one's friends. In short, the core ethical dispositions of the Judeo-Christian tradition are best nourished when (1) political activity in public life, (2) worship in a religious community, and (3) interpersonal dialogue on the meaning of faith for all of life *are found together in the lives of people.* Without exception we found that merely talking about public issues in the context of congregational life with-

ACTION POTENTIAL SCORES
by Political Involvement with Varied Social Context

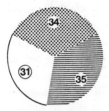

**Action Potential
General Population
Mean Scores**

High Political
Involvement
High Ethically
Oriented
Religious
Participation
High Friendship
Satisfaction

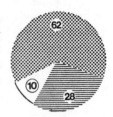

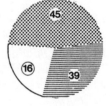

High Political
Involvement
Low Ethically
Oriented
Religious
Participation
High Friendship
Satisfaction

**High Political
Involvement**

Low Political
Involvement
Low Ethically
Oriented
Religious
Participation
Low Friendship
Satisfaction

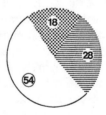

**Low Political
Involvement**

KEY: ▒▒▒ HIGH ≡≡ MEDIUM ☐ LOW

Figures shown are percentages.

RACIAL OPENNESS SCORES
by Political Involvement with Varied Social Context

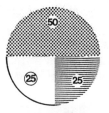

Racial Openness
General Population
Mean Scores

**High Political
Involvement
High Friendship
Satisfaction
High Ethically
Oriented
Religious
Participation**

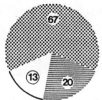

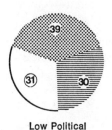

High Political
Involvement

**High Political
Involvement
Low Friendship
Satisfaction
Low Ethically
Oriented
Religious
Participation**

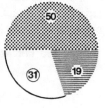

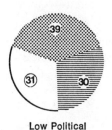

Low Political
Involvement

**Low Political
Involvement
Low Friendship
Satisfaction
Low Ethically
Oriented
Religious
Participation**

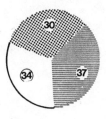

KEY: ▦ HIGH ≣ MEDIUM ☐ LOW

Figures shown are percentages.

out active involvement leads to a *lower* level of ethical maturity than is found in the public at large! Ethical sensitivity tends to accompany citizen activity whether or not the support of an issue-sensitive congregation is present. *But, above all, the marks of the church are strongest when these conditions are brought together.*

These findings constitute a dramatic confirmation of the Biblical description of the upbuilding ethic. The essential wisdom of this ethic is that the processes of building up *persons*, building up *community*, and building up *society* must be considered as facets of a *single task*. Practically speaking, the lack of any one dimension greatly weakens the other two. All three are vital for generating in persons the spiritual power for living out the Biblical ethic.

To summarize what we have perceived here: We have developed criteria for defining a group of modern urban citizens who will be predictably strong in:

1. Action Potential

> a disposition to act on their beliefs, a readiness to collaborate in tending to community needs.

2. Public Regard

> a willingness to act for the good of others or for the common good even when there is a sacrifice of private interests required.

3. Racial Openness

> an intellectual and emotional openness to the interests of all persons regardless of race, sex, age, nationality, or other arbitrary social boundaries.

4. Trust

> an affirmative disposition toward life which is given expression in mutually supportive friendship patterns and openness to the future, and is usually associated with emotional and physical well-being.

The language may still clash with the secular sensibilities of our time. But we believe that we have here an approximate measure for locating the People of God in the Raleigh–Durham–Chapel Hill area, or any area of American society. Like John Calvin we would be the last to claim that we are able to know who the "saved" are. That old curiosity had little to do with this inquiry. In an exceedingly rugged, empirical sense, we wanted to know what main *behaviors* could be associated with a style of religious life integrally continuous with that of people in the Bible. That life-style could be called the "ethical marks of the true church." Down through church history theologians have given only desultory attention to the identity of the church in *ethical* terms. In spite of Jesus' injunction, "By their fruits you will know them," the classic theology of the church has concentrated on such symbolic institutional marks as the preaching of the gospel and the administration of the Sacraments. Whether ethical behavior ought to be included as a mark of the very "being" or merely of the "well-being" of the People of God, we will not venture to say. But on this proposition we can be empirically emphatic: *The church, to maintain its own spirit and ethical vitality, must facilitate the involvement of local congregation members in political processes as well as talking about social issues.*

To the Biblical and historical study of the early chapters of this study we believe we have added an important empirical demonstration that the so-called split between private and public religion in the United States is profoundly contrary to the facts as well as the theological roots of the contemporary Christian church. But as distinctively flavored and worth savoring as this bit of evidence may be, it calls for much further understanding along two lines: (1) How do people develop in our culture into different styles of religious belief, church participation, ethical concern, and sociopolitical activity? (2) What strategies might church leaders devise for the encouragement of the style that overcomes the split between public and private religion?

An answer to the first question comprises Chapter 6; an answer to the second, Chapter 7.

Chapter 6

Becoming
Ethically Mature

Both science and religion begin with the conviction that there is explanation, meaning, coherence in human affairs. But science and religion differ in their assumptions about convincing evidence. What early Christians believed and did may not be as interesting to most sociologists as, for example, what living Christians believe and do. Adequate empirical tools for examining the first century are lacking from this perspective. Moreover, with their remarkable tolerance for incomplete answers or absence of answers, most scientists prefer an honest "We don't know" to a hopeful "We think so." Even here, however, one can make an unstrained analogy from the spirit of science to the spirit of Biblical faith: down through the ages Jews and Christians have seldom claimed absolute knowledge about anything —certainly not about God, nor about the mysteries of good and evil, nor about the total meaning of history. They *have* believed that vital, central clues for unraveling the basic plot of the human drama have been revealed in the drama. Christians read the "signs of the times" enough to get the gist of things. Though they will forever "see through a glass darkly," they do not live essentially in the dark. They have enough light from the past to illuminate much meaning in the present and to foreshadow much meaning still to come.

KIND HEARTS OR CLOSED MINDS?

Among the persons interviewed for the Urban Policy Study, we discovered those who have appropriated the ethical marks of God's people. This discovery offers a timely sign to those of us who seek to nourish ethical maturity in ourselves and our neighbors. In this chapter we ask a question that is at once theologically grounded and social-scientifically informed: "What critical psychological and social characteristics distinguish those who have combined citizen involvement with an ethical-religious perspective?" If we knew those characteristics, we would not necessarily know how to create certain kinds of people, any more than a farmer knows how to create potatoes. But a good farmer knows how to cultivate them, and he knows the difference between poor quality and high quality potatoes.

Such judgments seem inevitable in human history. When human beings stop making judgments on better and worse varieties of themselves, they will lose much of what we have called faith, meaning, religion, ethics.

Not to have some measures of better and worse in one's life, in fact, is to lack an identity. One of our large general interests in the Urban Policy Study was the process by which various Americans establish their identity within the tissue of expectations they entertain for themselves in relation to other people. We discovered in Chapter 5 a minority of people unique in their integration of individual self-consciousness and sensitivity to society. How did they manage this integration? Some further data from our study suggest an answer.

Apparently the frequent pattern in our society is for people to become identified with their role in a given social group or to seek individual identity without assuming much responsibility for the fate of others. Social pressures in communities and institutions are such that most people, insofar as they see alternatives, see an either/or choice between "being oneself" and "helping others." We had dramatic evidence of this condition when we asked a computer to analyze the personal characteristics of our 900 respondents. Like the efficient slave it is, the computer took everything we fed it—data on people's satisfaction with life at home, at work, among friends, and in their political activity; attitudes about helping others; open-mindedness and closed-mindedness; and attitudes toward institutions and social issues. Then, with the help of resourceful mathematicians, we asked the computer to tell us the simplest and most economical way to summarize all of these differences among the 900 people. The computer then came up with an answer at once very smart for the computer but very dumb for the society it had to describe with our data: The statistically most powerful and efficient way to categorize individual differences in the general population is to ask, Does a person acknowledge social dependence and accept mutual social obligations *or* has that person, instead, developed a strong sense of his or her individual identity? Persons who are strong in one of these sets of traits tend to be weak in the other, or so read the data.

Here is one strand in the mystery of American society which Christians, in particular, need to unravel. What are we to make of a society in which choices are frequently structured so that a person is forced to choose between personhood on the one hand and regard for the fate of one's neighbor on the other? From the perspective of the Pilgrim People of God, must not such a society be pathological? Apparently it poses to its members the *choice* between two virtues. In the realm of virtue, such a choice seems tragic. To be sure, we all have our favorite virtues—we differ considerably in whether we would prefer most to be healthy, wealthy, wise, open-minded, or compassionate. But few of us would choose only one such virtue, and only a fool sees any necessary opposition between health and wisdom. Our society apparently promotes foolishness systematically by opposing individuality and community.

The pervasiveness of this value-split in the general culture places all of our basic institutions under indictment. What is there about our educational system, our economic system, and our political system that promotes individuality at the expense of community? Consider, for example, the educational system. On the positive side, our research findings show that the level of educational attainment is strongly associated with a deepened sense of personal identity. Persons gain a greater sense of self-direction, a sense of personal control in their life, the more they participate in a formal educational system. In the process they also become more open-minded in relating to others with diverse values or divergent life-styles. They become more at home in a pluralistic global village, less racist, and less nationalistic. All this spells aid and comfort to teachers, professors, and college presidents.

Our study also documents negative events associated with education, however. The launching of an American's formal educational development starts in a setting that indirectly encourages individuals to break away from their family and their initial circle of friends.

Especially in schools, persons are directed into an individualized conception of their identity and destiny. They learn that on a normal curve one rises when others fall. There is little rising or falling together. Consequently there is a weakening of commitment to other people. The competitive structure of the system, insofar as it pits person against person, implicitly teaches, "Fend, first of all, for yourself!" Then, insofar as the educational system is also filled with caring people who want pupils to do their best, there is also a lesson about agreeing to be loners together.

But then there is the mirror-opposite group of people: helpers-of-neighbors who have minds closed to neighbors' opinions. As any good medical doctor or pastoral counselor knows, considerable listening to troubled persons may have to precede accurate diagnosis of their trouble. Helpfulness probably *needs* open-mindedness as its operational ally in many a human relationship. But something in our society makes these two strangers to each other. How does this happen? Again, the answer has to be complex. Apparently Henry David Thoreau was typically American (of the open-minded type) when he exclaimed that if he heard some person was about to visit him in order to do him some "good," he would quickly take his departure through a back window. The sage of Walden Pond was objecting, of course, to those characterological descendants of the Puritans who earned reputations as busybodies, imposing their help upon people who do not ask for it. Apparently Americans grow up amateurish in the art of combining a disposition to be helpful to the neighbor with a disposition of openness to the neighbor's contrary points of view. When you think about it, both peoples in Thoreau's remark are a caricature of Christian character: the Puritan know-it-all and Thoreau himself, the Yankee leave-me-alone. Anyone tempted to choose between these two should take a quick glance backward to that 1975 heart attack of Shirley Weatherford. Somebody's knowledge really did make a difference to her life, as did somebody's openness to finding out her real trouble. What help might she have received from "tolerant" neighbors who prefer to leave each other alone?

This backdrop of opposition between individuality and community enables us to focus more clearly on the uniqueness of that subpopulation of ethically mature persons discovered in the preceding chapter. More than any other group these persons seem to have resisted the influences that seduce Americans into sacrificing either personhood or social community. This group includes those members of church groups who, however mildly, criticize their own life-style in terms of a communal ideal and who also participate in politics. These people apparently practice a style of life that finds strength rather than threat in the interplay of individuality, intimacy, and public obligation. What most people choose between, this group manages to combine.

One general characteristic of the ethically mature, for example, is that they are likely to enjoy *both* a high level of satisfaction with their friends and a comparatively high level of physical health. They are the most likely persons to express agreement with statements like:

> "I can be sure that some of the friends I have will never turn their backs on me."
> "If I could not look after my family, my friends would see that they are taken care of."

And they are the most likely to say "not often" to questions like:

> "How often are you bothered by an upset stomach?"
> "How often do you have trouble getting to sleep and staying asleep?"

The striking thing in our finding is the interpendence of these characteristics. A person highly involved in politics and little involved in some form of "public" religion is much less likely to affirm friendship satisfaction and good health than the person who has both those former involvements. For the ethically mature, not only do "religion and politics mix" but they mix with health and friendship in mutually fortifying ways.

The sociologist Max Weber once defined the vocation of the politician as a "slow boring of hard boards."[1] When we remember the frustrations of people like Jeremiah, John Calvin, Louella McCabe, and Paul Ransom, it is obvious to us that political involvement on behalf of social justice involves facing some anguish along the way. The capacity to utilize the resources of a social group for regenerating energy, hope, and a sense of direction is essential to a People of God. Not only religious teachers but also family therapists and political philosophers are among those who have sought to cultivate this group potential. Simone Weil, Mahatma Gandhi, and Martin Luther King, Jr., have all pointed to the importance of loving human relationships for the function of transforming hurt into something other than a motive for revenge. Otherwise the victim of suffering is prompted to find relief by inflicting suffering on others. Richard Rabkin, M.D., of Community Research Application in New York, offers this analysis:

> The resilience of any system depends on its ability to transfer external challenges or absorb them. In the case of evil, a system may choose to pass on the evil to which it has been exposed, to seek revenge, as Charlie Company did (in the My Lai massacre). Or it may absorb it—as a system. To use a non-human example, a tidal marsh can absorb the enormous force of a hurricane because it is a spongy mass which bends with the storm and yields to its pressure. . . . In human social systems, mourning, when it involves the sharing of stress, is a very similar process. It is not the transfer of pain to a single martyr, or scapegoat, but a diffusion of the original pain. Grief, as the old saying goes, is itself a medicine, but not when the burden of pain must be borne alone.[2]

The reciprocal gift of such community is not less individuality but more. Friendships, church relationships, and political associations of the ethically mature seem to encourage them to combine assertions of their own personhood with sensitivity to other people. We discovered a similar combination of characteristics in these people in another part of our study which sought to determine the degree of open-mindedness and social helpfulness among our 900 respondents. For purposes of the study, an open-minded person was one who was likely to disagree with statements like:

> "There is only one right way to think about things."
> "There are two kinds of people: those who are for the truth and those who are against the truth."

And a person committed to common welfare is likely to agree with statements like:

"People who have a hard time with a problem have a right to expect help from others."

"When one group is rich and another is poor, it is the duty of the rich group to make things better for the poor."

Our data tell us that persons who combine an open mind and social helpfulness tend also to combine the four marks of ethical maturity. By contrast, those lacking *either* an open mind *or* social helpfulness *all* score markedly lower on the four ethical marks. In a profound sense, the ethically mature are those who "have it all together"—but "it" is a complex of intrapersonal, interpersonal, and public relationships not easy to achieve in our society. If these people were to transpose themselves into musical performers, they would be equally at home either as soloists or as members of an orchestra. Again, they combine the virtues that others choose between.

INDIVIDUALISM AND COMMUNITY IN HISTORICAL CONTEXT

We have seen in Chapter 4 how twentieth-century American culture had its immediate foundations in the history of nineteenth-century industrialism, frontier expansion, and religious revivalism. Rationalized by Adam Smith's philosophy, baptized by the Private side of the evangelical revivals, made alluring by the possibilities for personal wealth in a rich, new continent, and supported by the power of governments and industrial corporations, the Horatio Alger myth flourished mightily as the new century dawned. Many Americans born between 1900 and 1925 found the myth resonant with echoes from the life dream of their own parents. Many persons reading these pages will hear those echoes in their memory of their own public school experience during the first half of this century. Like publicly supported schools in every culture, America's schools have been financed and designed for the service of "majority views." The ability to criticize the role of the United States in world affairs, for example, is unlikely to be acquired in public schools.

More than uncritical nationalism, however, public school education has strongly contributed to the American expectation that everyone will be a "good competitor." Competition pervades the twelve

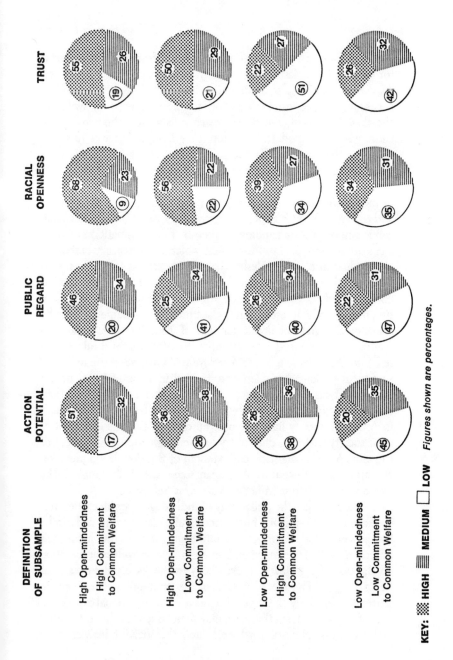

KEY: ░ HIGH ▦ MEDIUM ☐ LOW   *Figures shown are percentages.*

THE ETHICAL MARKS OF A PEOPLE OF GOD
as Related to the Integration
of Open-mindedness with Commitment to Common Welfare

grades of most school systems in this country from the first gold star for spelling to the last football trophy. Scholarship, teaching, athletics, money, clothes, sex, automobiles, and college applications are all occasions, in American high schools, for races between the swift and the slow. Life itself, the system teaches, is a race; the winners are those who work hardest. Therefore they have themselves to thank most for their success. By the same token, losers have themselves most to blame for their failures.

The cost of this individualism in American culture, like the cost of many other life-style choices, has been high for both the winners and the losers in the competitive system. For the winners, individualism is emotionally demanding. Achievement in competition requires a control of emotional expressiveness which was classically embodied in the dictum of John Wesley that his Methodist followers should "make all [the money] you can," and "save all you can." Only limited enjoyment of the pleasures of wealth is possible under this combination of rules, which resulted in the accumulation of large fortunes by some of the great capitalist families of America. Before he died Andrew Carnegie paid some attention to Wesley's third rule, which fell into disuse among some Wesleyans: "Give all you can." Less successful persons than Carnegie, trained in some of his character traits, must exact *more* self-repression from themselves the less their individual striving results in obvious success. In fact, such individuals in American society have a double burden to bear: the judgment of their society that they did not try hard enough and self-judgment of the same order. A dramatic embodiment of this double judgment on the mid-twentieth-century American stage was Willy Loman—the tragic hero of Arthur Miller's *Death of a Salesman.*[3]

Carried this far, the philosophy of individual-bears-all carries in it the seed of some similarly bitter social fruit. Blame of the self can be quickly converted, via projection, into blame of other people for their failures as well. Thus individualism has a logic as well as an emotion on the side of the view that everybody in the society deserves what he or she gets. The alleged victims of the "system"—poor people in particular—are only victims of themselves. The emotional expressiveness of black people, in this view, may then be seen as the trifling that defies the discipline of hard work, and the socialist insistence on

cooperation becomes a threat to freedom. That freedom and cooperation belong together is a strange and unorthodox thought to this
perspective.[4]

It should not surprise us, therefore, that we found evidence, paral-
leled by other recent social research on the American church, that
associates some church activity with racism. The Privatist side of
nineteenth-century evangelical Protestantism seldom promoted overt
hatred for persons of another race than one's own. It simply concentrated so exclusively upon individual religious experience and upon
striving for individual piety that it left the door of Protestant consciousness open to a natural temptation of capitalist culture to
"blame the victims." The victims might be urban workingmen who
would be a financial success if they abandoned the sins of drinking,
swearing, gambling, and joining unions.[5] Or they might be red people, technologically in the Stone Age, who had little success in stop-
ping the westward advance of white people. Had they been more
successful or had they fallen into white people's way of economic
industriousness, they might have qualified for the status of "good
Indians." As it was, given his own embodiment of the Westward-ho
spirit, Theodore Roosevelt was venting his own logic when, in a
moment of dreadful departure from the ethics of the Bible, he made
his famous remark:

> I don't go so far as to think that the only good Indians are the dead
> Indians, but I believe that nine out of ten are, and I shouldn't inquire too
> closely into the case of the tenth.[6]

With this remark Roosevelt undoubtedly brought chuckles from his
audience. The remark has been widely quoted since 1900. Seventy-
five years later, it would be simply the typical response of an individualist culture now to blame Roosevelt *himself* for his contemptuous
cruel humor. Better that we observe how he was an American of the
nineteenth century. His mid-nineteenth-century boyhood must have
been filled with many public statements akin to that of the New York
Presbyterian minister who said proudly in 1854:

> The English and the Scottish Puritans, the generous Hollanders, the
> Protestant Irish, and the noble Hugonots [sic] of France constitute the

elements of our national greatness. Never has the world seen four nobler races of men; races whose combined intelligence, piety, and thrift were so remarkably fitted by divine providence to convert these western forests into a great and growing empire.[7]

Any critique of American individualism must be qualified. Racial prejudice and nationalistic aggression both have many other causes. Also the individualist can find less destructive ways for dealing with psychological tensions that may be inherent in their life-style. Nevertheless, the tendencies for racism, sexism, and militarism to be associated with a general posture that is individualistic, reveres America uncritically, and explains problems in our society through blame for their victims were statistically significant in our random survey of 900 Americans undertaken as late as 1972 in central North Carolina.

We say "as late as 1972" because we have reason to believe that some fundamental changes are brewing below the surface of American life. One impressionistic index will be the reader's probable grimace at the ill-fated, oft-quoted Roosevelt remark about Indians. The remark sounds horrible to a *growing* number of Americans of all skin colors. If we had used the remark as an "item" in our Urban Policy Study, we would probably have secured a rejection response in the vicinity of 99 percent. The remark is too blatantly racist for most late-twentieth-century Americans to accept consciously anymore. A raft of books on the culture and history of the Indian, movies dramatizing the Indian point of view, and television narratives of heroic resistance to the U.S. Cavalry like that of Chief Joseph, all suggest that even white Americans have stopped smiling over the "dead Indian" business. Black Americans never did smile over it. Some white Americans, to the contrary, seem to be learning to cry, in retrospect, over that tragic business.

Any critique of American individualism must also be qualified by a tribute to the enormous achievement to which it contributed: the building of a country that had become, by the early twentieth century, the richest in the world. That individual effort only contributed to the achievement and did not simply produce it, any analysis of American economic history must certainly concede. Without the support of government and the exploitation of Chinese laborers, for example, the Western railroads would not have been built as soon or as numerously as they were. American culture makes it easy for most Americans to credit such achievements chiefly to striving individuals. That point our survey data bear out, as does much historical precedent reviewed in Chapter 4.

But our data also bear signs of a ground shift in our culture's individualist, economic-success-oriented ideals.

THE 1970's: BEYOND INDIVIDUALISM

One moral advantage of social research is that it opens the window a bit to the thinking of one's neighbors down the block. What if in increasing numbers they too are uncomfortable with their culture's shrill note of individualism? To discover *that* would make one feel less lonely, less a solitary voice crying in the wilderness.

One of the aims of the Urban Policy Study was to determine what impressions typical citizens have of their fellow citizens' opinions on major issues in contemporary American society. On a number of such issues we asked pairs of questions like this:

"Do you think the government should make sure that people who cannot afford health care can get free health care?"
"What proportion of people in the public do you believe probably favor the same thing?"

Over 93 percent of our 900 respondents answered yes to the first question, but "50 percent" was the average answer to the second— a large discrepancy. It suggests that on the issue of medical care *the typical citizen favors a social change for which far more support exists in the public at large than he or she suspects.*

The example is worth pondering. Louella McCabe's frustration with medical care facilities in Boston echoes the experience of many other city dwellers of all social classes. Some form of publicly subsidized health care appeals to a large public majority now, in spite of much devotion to privatized medicine. Although medical care is only an illustration of one break from the pattern of isolating "private care" from "public care" in American society, the illustration is eloquent with meaning. The more affluent Americans have become, the more they have been willing to spend on medical care. Both Louella McCabe and Shirley Weatherford benefited from that affluence. On the particular days they went to the hospital, each got comparatively "good" service. But Louella has experienced many other sorts of days; and if Shirley takes her children to a local hospital emergency room, she could easily have the experience which growing numbers of middle-class people have had: the experience of having their needs ignored. Because of rising expectations for health care and diminishing satisfaction with health care delivery, the American middle class is shifting its support toward greater governmental involvement in providing a better system. Experience, not only moral argument or economic ideology, accounts for this shift. Increasing numbers of people understand firsthand the frustrations that Louella and her nonaffluent neighbors have undergone during most of their urban lives.

A simple way of describing such experience would be: *Americans are learning that rugged individuals need rugged social support.* Popular discussion of socialized medicine is only one sign of large-scale cultural changes that are detected more systematically in recent research like the Urban Policy Study. Several generalizations growing out of these studies will help to describe the changes:

1. *Affluent societies inevitably "suffer" from rising expectations.* By standards widely accepted in twentieth-century America, John Calvin lived in a gruesomely primitive medieval city. In the lifetime of many of us, we have all grown accustomed to living in a city with a pure water supply, disease-free sewage disposal, inoculations for the prevention of epidemics, prewarnings about impending natural disasters like hurricanes, instant electronic communications, and a host of other services. These are made available from a combination of governments, private businesses, and voluntary agencies. All of them are possible partly because of enormous accessions of knowledge, organization, and money which, in the Geneva of John Calvin, would have seemed utterly fantastic. Many Americans compare their own lifestyle with that of the home in which they grew up one generation ago. In the quarter century since 1950, for example, we have doubled our national per capita consumption of beef. The economic support of our new expectations obviously comes through two major funnels:

personal income and public expenditures. The more money one makes, the more "needs" one discovers, and the more complex each new need tends to be. A well-known contemporary psychologist, Abraham Maslow, has theorized that human beings have a hierarchy of such needs built from basic "survival" (enough food to keep you from dying) to "security" (enough in the pantry to keep you from worrying) to "affection" (your associates love you) to "self-esteem" (you love yourself) to "self-actualization" (you become everything you are capable of becoming). Whether these five are just the right needs or rightly arranged by Maslow may be argued. Hardly arguable is the fact that both persons and societies, as they become more affluent, invent needs which previous generations considered luxuries. As Dwight McDonald said, in an article on America's "invisible poor" in 1963, in America "not to be able to afford a movie or a glass of beer is a kind of starvation—if everybody else can."[8]

2. *Members of affluent societies are more likely therefore to suffer from identity failure than from gross economic failure.* The word "identity," in its psychological sense, has become an ordinary word in conversation in this country partly through the writings of Erik Erikson.[9] Doctors report more visits to their offices by persons suffering from nonphysical complaints than from physical.[10] The crises on university campuses in the late '60s suggested to many ministers and counselors that the demands of young Americans for social recognition as unique persons (as opposed to a role title like "Mother" or "plumber") increased more rapidly than did the social pathways through which persons could establish such an identity. Consequently our society now suffers from a condition new in the history of mankind: a majority of persons who, in varying degrees, identify themselves as failures! According to our survey, few classify themselves as insecure in terms of food-in-the-pantry images. The pioneer American—from the rockbound Puritan to the sod-busting Midwesterner—was always a crop away from starvation. This is still true of the majority of humans living on this planet. But the Americans who spoke to us in the Urban Policy Study complain, not of economic hardship, but of loneliness, ineffectiveness in their work, and impotence in their political relationships. Such data fit exactly the medical testimony that patients these days complain more of identity failures

than of physical maladies. Attesting to this is the huge demand for tranquilizers which doctors and druggists dispense daily.

3. *Identity failure calls for the remedy of new relationships to one's fellow humans.* Erik Erikson has insisted that personality comes to birth in us all by a series of lifetime negotiations with our historic ancestors, our parents, our peers, and a widening circle of other human beings. None of Maslow's hierarchy of needs gets satisfied outside some network of individual give-and-take with other individuals. Many in America seem to have discovered that in the inventive fumbling which was called by some "the counterculture." Sociologist Patrick Conover suggests that it should more accurately be called the invention of an "alternative culture." These were the people who set up alternative medical clinics on the streets of San Francisco, formed underground churches, connected telephone hot lines for troubled runaways and drug users, organized over three thousand communes, and formed perhaps as many as forty thousand "intentional communities" across the United States. Many of the communes in urban settings, reports Conover, make it possible for their members to eat meals with several nuclear families, to send their children to a free school, to get help at a free clinic, and to attend an underground church while holding jobs found through an "alternative employment" directory which specializes in human service.[11] The proliferation of these experiments tells us something about the way a certain segment of our national population is seeking to cope with their sense of identity failure: *by a search for increased social cohesiveness.*

4. *Americans' current search for a new social identity usually does not break radically with a measure of affluence.* To the contrary, the glorification of poverty has little place among the architects of the cultural experiments just sketched. A university professor was conversing in the late 1960's with a young woman in San Francisco's Haight-Ashbury district. He asked her, "How do you and your friends get bread to eat?" In apparently sincere amazement, the woman replied: "Bread? Why worry about bread? Bread just *is.*" Naive the reply may sound to ears trained to the sounds of the Great Depression, or infuriating to two thirds of the world's people who go to bed hungry; but the answer was not irrational for a person born in 1950. For such a person the "problem" of American agriculture was always

surplus. Television advertisements have always made the buying of many products less basic than bread seem a patriotic duty. (The average American high school graduate of the '70s, one writer estimates, has seen 350,000 television advertisements, most of them urging consumers to engage in some form of surplus buying.)[12] Even the poverty of the counterculture assumed the indispensability of rock music via stereo. And unless we agree that humanity *should* live "by bread alone" (a philosophic claim that can easily be read into both Karl Marx and Adam Smith), why should we protest the liberation which some Americans feel in having bread to eat *while* they enjoy recorded music? On all sides we are thus reminded that we live in an affluent society. Long ago we began our pilgrimage beyond survival values toward those "higher order values" which, however difficult to describe and rank, must be associated with human nature and human history. This introduces an empirical note into Jesus' claim about our not living by bread alone. We humans have never lived *only* for enough food to keep us alive. In those situations where we can count on enough food, we go on to work on projects that are only possible for people who do not have to spend all their time "bringing home the bacon." What but an affluent, meat-eating society would invent a colloquial term for survival that utilized the word "bacon"?

5. *The sometimes violent clamor for social change in recent American history has erupted, then, not merely from deepening despair but from escalating hope as well.* This generalization can be overstated; but as leaders of soldiers, revolutionaries, and political reform movements can testify, hopeless people make bad recruits to a cause. Little Oliver Twist does not ask for "more" a second time when his experience teaches him that the request is hopeless. There is some reason, therefore, to make the claim: the civil rights movement, the women's liberation movement, the massive protests over the Vietnam war, and the quest for alternative institutions in the '60s all emerged when they did for good reason. It was not because our culture was becoming more racist or more sexist or more militaristic and socially callous, but because we were becoming significantly less so. How much less is hard for anyone to calculate. A society whose conservatives, liberals, and radicals all continue to find a good press in social evil makes the

celebration of social good a risky intellectual task. Church historian Sydney Ahlstrom sees the 1960's as marking the end of the age of the white Anglo-Saxon Protestant dominance in American culture.[13] It also marks the emergence into American political life of those robust minorities whose voices have long been suppressed in national affairs. Had Martin Luther King, Jr., been born in the generation of Booker T. Washington, he might have suffered with Washington the insult of a President who spoke of black people as "a race altogether inferior to whites" and confessed publicly that he erred in inviting Washington to the White House as a dinner guest.[14]

Think about it. We have come *from* a time when the legacy of slavery carried over into the complete absence of black people from national political affairs *to* a time when in seven years (1965–1972) the number of black elected officials in the American Deep South increased from 50 to 1,100. An eminent black congresswoman was keynote speaker in a 1976 national party convention, and an equally eminent black congressman now represents the American people in the United Nations. Black voters are credited with the margin of power that was needed to elect the first white Southeastern President of the country in 112 years. We have come *from* a time when racist jokes about black people and Indians were good public entertainment *to* a time when they are at most tolerated. Nine out of ten respondents in Raleigh, Durham, and Chapel Hill, North Carolina, will affirm—at least in a confidential interview—that neither race is better than the other. We have come *from* a time when a war to make the world "safe for democracy" commanded the near-religious enthusiasm of Americans *to* a time when millions of Americans learned to swallow the truth spoken by thousands of students that some national wars are not worth fighting. We have come *from* a time when a prominent Protestant minister of the 1920's could commend "woman" as "the mere dependent and ornament of man in his happier hours"[15] *to* a time when 6 in 10 citizens among our 900 say that more women should seek political office. The resistance that greeted some of these changes in the '60s and '70s in America tells us how far the nation has yet to go before it achieves an acceptable level of justice. But history tells us also how far we have come, and how differently the word "acceptable," in some dimensions of our culture, is now defined.

6. *An affluent society, therefore, can afford to raise large questions of social justice and compassion in ways that a poorer society may not afford.* The word "afford" is slippery. But it is undeniable that both capitalist and socialist countries now exemplify rising popular expectations concerning the specifics of "justice" in their respective societies. Evidence from the Urban Policy Study suggests that this generalization rings true of individuals as well as of societies as a whole. Americans in the colonial era, for example, could not afford to consider compulsory public schooling very seriously, any more than the typical American farmer could afford to send a son to Harvard. Public schooling and even a college education are available now to an unprecedented number of young Americans.

The truth of this generalization is evident in our study. To test our respondents' perception of their overall sense of economic security, we asked them about the adequacy of their money income and the houses they lived in. We then looked at that group who had best combined "Open-mindedness" with "Commitment to Others." (This group, remember, had like high scores on our four marks of ethical maturity.) The graph on page 132 details the results.

This finding tells us something that undermines myths to the right and to the left in modern economic ideologies: Against the hard-work myth of capitalism, it is *not* true that to be poor in this society is to lack ethical maturity. Persons with low levels of economic security can combine the traits of a high level of such maturity—if not, the line at the left on the chart would rise steeply from 0 percent. But against the Marxist myth of the self-satisfied bourgeoisie, it *is* true that the higher your personal economic security in American society the more you are likely to be concerned *and* engaged with the cause of social justice for the neglected people of the society; the more, in fact, you are likely to be concerned not only with charity but with the change of economic-political structures to overcome deficiencies of justice.

To support this surprising claim, here is a sample of the questions our respondents had to answer concerning their opinions about major national political issues. (In general the population randomly sampled does not have a record of being more liberal than other parts of the country. Our questions covered human services, economic inequities,

Percentage of Respondents
with Combination of High Scores
on Open-mindedness and Commitment to Others

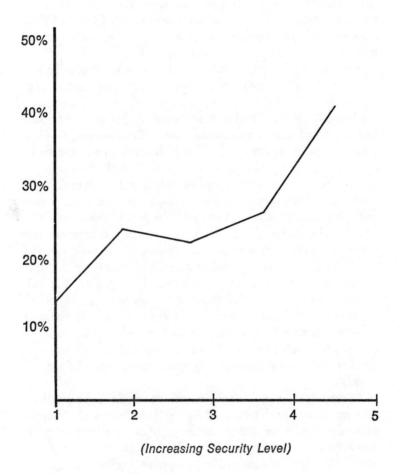

(Increasing Security Level)

and racial openness. The number of people sampled on each item is above 900.)

	Yes	No	Not Sure
Do you think the government ought to guarantee a living to those who cannot find work?	62.8%	34.8%	2.4%
Do you think the government should make sure that people who cannot afford health care can get free health care?	93.5%	5.1%	1.4%
Do you think all get their fair share of money to live on?	17.0%	76.3%	6.7%

	Fair and Wise	Major Change	Other
On the whole, do you think our present economic system is fair and wise, or do you think we have to make major changes?	22.8%	62.0%	15.2%

Respondents were given a circle graph—a "sliced pie"—showing how much all governments in the United States spend proportionately for different kinds of programs. Then they were asked:

	More	Same	Less	Not Sure
Do you think the governments should spend more, or less or about the same as they do now on defense?	3.1%	16.2%	73.3%	8.4%
Do you think the governments should spend more, or less, or about the same as they do now on education?	62.5%	30.3%	3.6%	3.6%

	Blacks Better	Whites Better	Both Same	Not Sure
Do you think black people are basically better than white people, or white people are basically better than black people, or most people are basically the same regardless of their race?	1.4%	7.1%	88.8%	2.7%

	Quite a Bit	Some- what	Not at All	Not Sure
How strongly would you object if a member of your family wanted to bring a white (black) friend home to dinner? Would you object quite a bit, somewhat, or not at all?				
Whites	20.3%	18.4%	59.9%	3.3%
Blacks	6.3%	15.6%	72.9%	5.0%

Answers to a number of these questions helped to determine a respondent's composite score on Racial Openness, Commitment to Others, and Public Regard. What stands out in the survey statistics here is *the clear association of higher levels of economic security with higher scores on ethical maturity.* Given the political changes posed in these questions, this means a willingness on the part of the individual to make personal economic sacrifices to put into effect these preferences. The overall finding does not permit us to make the broad, reverse generalization, "Affluent people are more ethically mature," but only that the minority of ethically mature people in all income groups is a larger minority among the affluent than among the poor.

In this qualified sense, then, we must conclude that affluence created in America under the pressures of a highly individualistic culture exerts some pressure, in turn, upon that very individualism. But at this point we must introduce a sober reflection from contemporary history that muddies the optimism which seems to flow from our research analysis here. With an economic recession barely and perhaps only temporarily over as this is written in 1977, some scholars are saying that the age of American affluence is over. Are the economic supports for realizing justice deteriorating just when a vision of justice glimmers on the horizon of popular consciousness?

THE 1980's: BEYOND AFFLUENCE

Those who argue the end of American affluence have a maze of contemporary fact on their side. They have a lot of both American and global history.

"Affluence" ("flowing toward") suggests the image of a river flowing effortlessly toward the sea.[16] In economic usage it refers to a conflux of riches incommensurate with sacrifices of labor, capital, or time. Since shortly after the founding of the colonies, America has normally been characterized by affluence. As Terrence McCarthy describes it,

> There was, even before the Revolution, a swelling inflow of capital, technology, manpower, and—the seizure of land from the Indians— seemingly unlimited natural resources for capital and labor jointly to exploit. There was a whole continent for the taking.[17]

Up until our present economic crisis, scarcity, when it appeared, was due to a lack of production, never to a lack of resources. Especially in the past quarter century, most American families have become accustomed to constantly increasing annual incomes. When average family income dropped 3.3 percent in 1974 from 1973, it was an event without precedent since 1949.[18]

The tide of affluence has come in many forms. Besides rich natural resources, there were technological advances in agriculture permitting manyfold increases in production. There were timely influxes of

foreign capital and, just before World War II, a huge inflow of
refugee gold from Europe.[19] There have been decades of inequitable
trade arrangements with countries of the Third World. In 1950–
1965, for example, U.S. companies put 9 billion dollars into Latin
America and took out nearly 26 billion in profits.[20] In 1969, when
the extraction of Middle East oil cost sixteen cents a barrel, the price
was set by the oil companies at the American cost of production, i.e.,
$1.75 a barrel.[21] It was perhaps this artery of cheap energy more than
any other single factor which financed this century's third-quarter
tide of affluence not only for the United States but also for Europe
and Japan.[22] The use of petroleum relative to other fuels in the U.S.
economy went from 14 percent fifty years ago, to 33 percent in 1950,
to over 60 percent in the '70s.[23] By 1973 the United States, with 6
percent of the world's population, was consuming one third of the
world's total energy output, at a cost of only 4 percent of its gross
national product.[24]

The era of this sort of U.S. affluence is, for the most part, over. The
floating of the dollar on the world market, the switch from a buyer's
to a seller's market for world resources, and the advance of cost-free
pollution to the limits of environmental tolerance all mean that the
United States both in transactions with the rest of the world and with
nature will henceforth have to give commensurately with what it
receives. The end of affluence by no means implies that America is
no longer a rich country. Nor does it mean that we cannot continue
to improve the quality of our economic system. It does mean that
ever-escalating production and consumption no longer provide "a
way out" to resolve economic dilemmas and social tensions. A constantly expanding economic "pie" is not the key to more social justice
for poor Americans. Neither is it the likely solution to the problem
of making a larger share of earth's limited resources available to the
mass of poor people around the globe.

We misread the signs of the times in America, however, if we see
our affluence as being only under attack by the price systems of world
markets. A grim internal attack also afflicts us. There is a growing split
between the people who benefit most from our national affluence and
the people who benefit least. One of the most pathetic stories to grow
out of the urban riots of 1968 (following the assassination of Martin
Luther King, Jr.) came from the city of Detroit: A shoe shop was

being looted by a young black man when the owner of the shop pulled up to the store in his car. The young man emerged from the store clutching in his hand a pair of shoes and two pairs of shoelaces. Taking out his shotgun, the storeowner shot the thief dead. Pictures in the newspaper from the same weekend showed other looters carrying off television sets and suits of clothes. Though the buildings burned down were located mostly in Detroit's black community, the story adds up to a terrible criticism of American affluent society. Triggered by the death of one of their great modern heroes, many poor black people in the cities experienced the death of hope, and in outraged despair they struck out at the nearest symbols of an affluence that they largely did not share. In counter anger and for the protection of property as trivial as shoelaces, some owners of that property struck back murderously, as more would be willing to do if our cities should again become battlegrounds between the haves and the have-nots.

Certain sections of Detroit had again turned into battlegrounds in the summer of 1976 when William Serrin, a journalist who has been writing about the city for over a decade, described Detroit as perhaps "the first dead large city" in the United States. In terms of unconcealed rage and despair, Serrin wrote of "hoodlums controlling many streets . . . people held up . . . homes broken into . . . people murdered . . . street after street lined with abandoned, vandalized stores." But his description concluded with a bitter rebuke to Detroit as a city that symbolizes what has been wrong with American society for a hundred years. His rebuke to our culture needs to stand alongside the hopeful improvements which our own Urban Policy Study detected. Serrin sees the excessive individualism and materialism of our national heritage as yielding poisonous fruit in this city where Henry Ford acquired the capacity to put a car in every American driveway.

> Taking the money and running is an old game in this country. It was not invented by the black gangs on the Detroit East Side. Old Henry Ford took his money and ran to Dearborn a long time ago, and the big merchants in downtown Detroit have been doing it for years. This is the way this nation was built. This is a country of selfish people seeking money and comfort. This is what is wrong in Detroit and that is what is wrong in this country.[25]

Such commentary does not tell the whole story of Detroit or any other part of urban America. It does not mention the decision of the Ford Motor Company, for example, to move the suburban offices of 2,700 of its employees back to the heart of downtown Detroit in 1977. But Serrin's rage must be kept much in the minds of ethically mature Christian Americans as they hope for a society of cities less "dimmed by human tears" than the ones we currently live in. Consider the willingness of many people who live in the newer cities of Houston and Los Angeles to let the New York Cities and Detroits "suffer for their sins" without benefit of federal aid. The lesson from those older cities is that without a quantum leap in justice for the poorer members of our entire society, even our current level of affluence may turn to bitter ashes. The pursuit of additional affluence will then become increasingly meaningless. *The threat is not only the deterioration of economic support for our values but the absence of values sufficient to manage our affluence.* Sociologist Robert Bellah puts this principle in terms scarcely less ominous than those of William Serrin:

> That happiness is to be attained through limitless material acquisition is denied by every religion and philosophy known to man but is preached incessantly by every American television set. What this does to the large portion of our population who have the resources to engage in the getting game is bad enough. What it does to millions who are marginal to our economy and can participate only vicariously in the great cornucopia is grim indeed, grim in inner disappointment and frustration, grim in the possibility of unrestrained violence. Few societies could imagine themselves surviving very long when one of their central institutions was advocating unrestrained greed. Are we so different from all other human societies?[26]

People who talk this way have critically important truth on their side. The point can be pressed more prudentially. National policies which emphasize increasing production and consumption—as the means to national prosperity and contentment—may or may not succeed in the short run. No one is really in a position to predict. Over the longer haul, however, such policies can only lead to exacerbated competitiveness and aggression centered around scarce resources. Even if the wealthy temporarily retrench to maintain their material advantages, they will suffer increasingly tense relationships with the poor of this nation and of the world. The issue is not whether postaffluence is coming, but how we will deal with it: with foresight and ethical wisdom or with denial and unwitting self-destructiveness.

Let us be clear about discriminating between the opportunities lost and those which are not with the coming of postaffluence. *What we are losing is an experience of the psychological and spiritual dead ends associated with a life centered on materialistic striving. We do not lose our opportunity to amplify the positive incentives in our social structures that can encourage people's psychological and ethical maturation through self-investment in meaningful activities.*

Our crying deficit of activities with personal-social meaning, rather than activities which merely add to the gross national product, can be illustrated profusely from everyday data of our lives. A recent advertisement from a major American oil company looks optimistically into the future of the American and the world economy through the eyes of the Hudson Institute, which predicts a rise in the personal income "of every man, woman, and child on earth . . . from a current $1,300 a year to $20,000." The Institute, we are told, "has a novel theory. It feels that the very gap that now separates the 'haves' from the 'have-not' nations will stimulate worldwide progress toward a future of economic abundance. The larger the gap, the Institute feels, the stronger the incentive for achieving a higher standard of living for all." Leaving aside the moral implausibility here ("let us have more injustice to achieve more justice") and leaving to economists and environmentalists the task of assessing the technical possibilities for billions of people to live on earth's resources at the rate Americans live on them, one passes incredulously to the last paragraph of this advertisement, which teases us with a few details on the technology of the world-affluent future:

> *Coming up.* Instead of stepping into your bathtub or shower, someday you'll enter a "people washer egg" that bathes, rinses, and dries you. For people who sew: you'll soon be able to forget the annoying snags that occur when you use certain fabrics. The ultrasonic machine of the future will weld seams rather than stitch them. And for those with self-doubt,

Dr. [Stephen] Rosen forecasts a scientific method for measuring romantic love.[27]

The best response to this apparently serious advertisement is a simple question to every reader: Do you *will* such a future? We might have used *this* small paragraph as a "test item" in our Urban Policy Study. Which of our 900 respondents would find this bit of futurology exciting, interesting, depressing, or enraging? How would you respond?

Around what human purposes shall we organize economic affluence? Quite a different answer to this basic theological-ethical question can be found in a novel by Walker Percy, *Love in the Ruins.* The story is a futurological autobiography of Dr. Tom More, a medical doctor living in Louisiana in an indefinite year of perhaps 2000. Dr. More might have begun his story sitting in downtown Detroit of 1976:

> Now in these dread latter days of the old violent beloved U.S.A. and of the Christ-forgetting, Christ-haunted, death-dealing Western world I came to myself in a grove of young pines and the question came to me: has it happened at last? . . .
>
> Is it that God has at last removed his blessing from the U.S.A. and what we feel now is just the clank of the old historical machinery, the sudden jerking ahead of the roller-coaster cars as the chain catches hold and carries us back into history with its ordinary catastrophes, carries us out and up towards the brink from that felicitous and privileged siding where even unbelievers admitted that if it was not God who blessed the U.S.A., then at least some great good luck had befallen us, and that now the blessing or the luck is over, the machinery clanks, the chain catches hold, and the cars jerk forward?[28]

Before the novel is over, Percy has delivered devastating comeuppance to a wide range of us who count ourselves citizens of these United States: technologists who forget the meaning of a human life apart from technology; social scientists who devise questionnaires to measure with finality "the soul of Western man";[29] medical researchers who love truth rather than people; businessmen who make money only to spend it on guns to protect their houses from the "Bantus"; and ministers who observe blandly, while living in a collapsing soci-

ety, that "Jesus was not a social reformer" yet making room for
gratitude for an "electric carillon that can be heard for five miles."[30]
Percy's bizarre, trivialized future America lacks an ultrasonic seam-
welder and a people-washer egg, but it does indeed have as one of its
key technical gadgets "a scientific method for measuring romantic
love." Somehow Percy's description of that gadget—"cameras whir,
tapes jerk around, needles quiver, computers wink"[31]—smites us two
social researchers with due humility about *our* craft too. He brings
us up short with the message our own book began by preaching: For
every little story you try to act or tell, look to the larger story of what
it all means! Either the head of the advertising department has failed
to care about setting that oil company in the framework of a larger
story, or that story has to be radically different from the one that
Christian Americans want to tell about their country. Who among
ethically mature Christians in the land can contemplate those in-
dexes of progress as anything but the hideous playing out of affluence
gone to dry leaf which has lost its roots in a profound interpretation
of the human drama?

We repeat: The end of *this* version of affluence cannot be hastened too quickly in America. But what if the end could be coupled
with new versions of the old ethic that requires us to "love our
neighbors as ourselves"? Some remnant of the old Puritan neighbor
regard is still left in many corners of our society. New murmurs of
public regard are stirring in an affluent body politic. With a still-
enduring amalgam of Biblical universalism and eighteenth-century
humanism which partly motivated the American Revolution, contemporary Americans might yet rescue their country from its jerky
descent, like an undirected roller coaster, into the oblivion of a rich,
self-centered, trivial, dehumanized existence.

What specific challenges are we raising here to ourselves and,
especially, to our friends and colleagues in the Christian churches of
this country? The answer to this question is the burden of our last
chapter, where we dwell not so much on the analysis of our Urban
Policy data nor upon the meaning of that data in the context of our
national culture, but upon pragmatic steps that an ethically mature
people, heirs of the Biblical faith, should be willing to take in response
to such an analysis.

Chapter 7

The People of God
in Urban America

The two persons from Chapter 1 most likely to pick up this book are Philip Delaney and Paul Ransom. One of them has implicitly promised to read it by urging us to write it. Now we come to the payoff chapter for the pragmatic mind: What do we do now? The Delaneys and the Ransoms do not fall for the pragmatism that *only* asks this question, only flips to the bottom line of action. They know that the Bible and Martin Luther were empirically correct to believe that "the righteous shall live by faith"; that soils of belief and trust nourish every significant human action; that history both limits and releases its inheritors for their own work as makers of history. How we spend the best years of our lives is a philosophical question before it becomes a pragmatic one.

Delaney and Ransom share profoundly an awareness of the Big Picture of which their lives are a part. By their education, experience, and affluence they are predictable candidates for our cluster of ethically mature Americans. One sign of that maturity, we remember, is Public Regard. These two men have obvious reason to rank high on this particular attitude. One has a personal goal of contributing, through his profession as a banker, to international peace and justice. The other has a similar goal as a high-ranking federal bureaucrat. However, both men have reached a point in their lives when their very acquaintance with the Big Picture gives them pause, afflicts them with anxiety, brings them up short. Should we any longer expect our society to embody our personal ideals?

This poignant question has an equally poignant inversion: Should we expect our personal ideals to embody our society anymore? To answer no to *either* question is an index to personal alienation and social disintegration. To answer yes to *both* seems to be the prescriptive requirement growing out of everything we have tried to say in these pages. In mature persons and societies, both the big and little pictures make sense, fortify each other's reality, and contribute to each other's fulfillment. A person who neglects responsibility to a steadily widening network of other persons is to the extent of that neglect less than human. A society that neglects its responsibility to the least of its individual members is to the extent of that neglect less than human.

But there is a qualification to this reaffirmation of the faith dimension of human existence. The righteous cannot live by faith alone, if by faith we mean a steadily held, strong-minded, interior spiritual tilt. Such individuals, our data overwhelmingly indicate, are likely candidates for lives of quiet desperation. Without the links of friendship, a worshiping community, a community for political discourse, and associates for their public action, the faithful are also the frustrated. Their righteousness has pale resemblance to the human vigor we glimpse in Jeremiah, Peter, Lydia of Philippi, Francis of Assisi, John Calvin, and Martin Luther King, Jr. Indeed, such sinner-saints among the People of God in history stand not as solitary heroes and heroines but as members of a communion of saints whose number vastly exceeds the samples that pepper history books. In that fact glimmers a promise by which every member of the People of God lives: the promise that a single person, joined and supported by other persons, can make at least an anonymous fingerprint on the Big Picture of human history itself. Behind us all are the precedents of Israel, the early church, the monastic reformers of the Middle Ages, the reformers who settled the New World, and the bands of reformers of today's church. The saints of God are launched on a pilgrimage that perpetually connects their little life story with the life stories of expanding numbers of other human beings. A Roman humanist said, "Nothing human is alien to me." With due recognition of those evil "human" things which must be striven against in the common life of us all, the People of God say the same for themselves. They believe that God has already said just that for himself in Israel, in Jesus, in the church, and in every other sign of his Kingdom.

Whoever we are, the complex stage on which we act threatens the most mature of us. Nobody can be blamed for wanting to cry out:

"Stop this world of urban decay, national bureaucracy, and world hunger. I want to get off!" In the hope that you will not in fact get off, in your mind or in your life, we have to recall a sobering fact: the slowness of 215 million Americans to learn from history, to read the meaning of their experience, and to reform their personal-social lives accordingly. The burden of our message over the past fifty pages has been moderately encouraging about the possibilities of beneficial change in the future. We have identified a strong minority of Americans who appropriate the understanding and the faith necessary for such change. But before one decides to cast one's lot with this minority, how do we set this positive evidence in the context of other admittedly negative evidence so that the one is not overwhelmed by the other? To answer this question is to state the case for joining minority movements which are the "right" movements in every major sense of that term.

The question can be restated this way: During the very months when our Urban Policy Study was proceeding in North Carolina, American voters, including North Carolinians, elected Richard M. Nixon as President of the country by an impressive majority. Rejected in this election was a Democrat who claimed that his religion, his voting record in the U.S. Senate, and his sense of national need impelled him to favor such things as government-guaranteed health care, the expenditure of more public money on education, less on defense, and the reform of economic inequities in American society. Our Urban Policy Study documented general support of just such changes among a majority of citizens in central North Carolina. *How then did the political opinion of a people desiring precisely these things get translated into power for an administration bent on economizing on such services while increasing defense expenditures?*

The question invites ethically mature citizens to see clearly the mix of political obstacle and pathway for a national move from attitude change to policy change. Just this mix of obstacle and pathway informed Paul Ransom's bureaucratic dream. What *are* the keys that will unlock the riches of the affluent and postaffluent society for the benefit of all its members? A foray into the analysis of how politics "work" in this country may be helpful preparation for framing an answer.

POWER-BROKERAGE AND PUBLIC APATHY

There are two levels on which the answer may be framed. The first is the process of power-brokerage by which the nation allocates that fifth of our gross national product spent by the Federal Government. The second is more psychological: the constraints which the average citizen feels upon his or her ability to exert influence on such areas of public policy.

1. John K. Galbraith and others have described elaborately the process that minimizes public input into the budgeting process of the Federal Government.[1] The clearest example of such minimal input, perhaps, is that of national defense weapons procurement. Like many other issues of policy in a technological society, weapons policy originates with ideas that only a technical elite knows enough to generate. What does the public know about missile systems, nuclear aircraft carriers, fighter aircraft, and manned bombers? Procurement decisions often begin in a weapons firm and in a particular military service for which the item is intended.[2] A common interest—the one in profit and the other in power—binds the two agencies together. When a military service defines a need for a product, often with the help of the weapons firm, both stand to gain. For example, in late 1976 a newspaper columnist asked the question:

> Why did a $15 million item for the Navy's F–14 fighter plane engine slip through the 1977 federal budget, with its destined impact of 1½ to 2 billion a year in future budgets?
> "Because [he answered] the Navy wanted its cherished engine, Grumman needs to build more F–14's, Pratt and Whitney coveted the engine contract . . . and the members of Congress who put through the appropriation wanted jobs for their constituencies."[3]

Such bureaucratic symbiosis of the Department of Defense with its patrons gets further support in the career patterns of their respective professional leaders, who move from positions in one to positions in the other with the ease of transferable expertise.[4] As Max L. Stackhouse has defined this pervasive interface of public-private bureaucracy:

> That system generates its own definition of needs and mobilizes its own resources to meet those needs. If one must identify a single image to

capture the nature of this phenomenon, it cannot be corrupt generals or businessmen, "merchants of death," "power elite," the whole of society, or the technostructure of corporations. If anything, the Military-Industrial Complex can only be compared in richness and complexity to a modern metropolis. Indeed, it is in some ways more complex and post-urban; for it is freed from any specific geographical boundary and it has greater technological-managerial capacity than any contemporary metropolis.[5]

Currently Congress and a new President promise some change in all this, yet recent historical precedent has inclined the President and the Armed Services Committee to accept without question the budget requests of the Department of Defense. Thus, decisions about relative allocations between defense and domestic welfare spending have been subject to a minimum of public opinion. As Stackhouse cautions, the military-industrial complex is no simple monolith of power. Inside the complex, titanic struggles go on between industries, the several armed services, and bureaucratic suboffices.[6] Sometimes the competition between these elements may even yield to a common solicitude for some one of them in distress. A case in point was government subsidy to a bankrupt Lockheed Aircraft Corporation. But the competition of viewpoints inside the structure in fact is narrow. Public interest consciousness that might exercise broader vision and authority over an agency of our society which possesses the power literally to destroy all societies in the world is relatively absent.

By way of bureaucratic contrast, it is no mystery why housing, health care, and education bear the brunt of economizing impulses in any presidential administration. Defense is one area of national policy in which central government exercises a virtual monopoly. Given the enormous sophistication and expense of modern military systems, only national governments have financial power to mount such systems. On the other hand, public need for housing, health care, and education gets tended largely by local agencies. Locally based governments, businesses, and professions spend most of the money and make most of the policy decisions. Housing, for example, including public housing, gets built by a network of contractors, land developers, and builders all tied into local decision-making centers. Insofar as better housing claims the budgetary help of city governments, such help remains tragically limited. The Federal Government has been a chief source of funds for housing elderly and low-income persons in the cities of the nation. When, as in the early '70s, a President exercises power to cut such funding—sometimes with a veto that overrides the vote of over half of the Congress—the construction of local public housing may cease in the very midst of putting up the roofs. Most of the public services associated with the amenity and the deterioration of life in a large American city stand in a similar position vis-à-vis sources of government funding. At the city level funds are scarcest and demands are greatest for public education, relief of starvation, protection of life and property against crime, arrest of pollution, and carrying away of garbage.[7]

The question of why American citizens feel alienated from influence on policy-making in the Department of Defense is thus easy to answer. Much harder to answer is why citizens surrounded by these locally visible and locally tended problems have not pressured and strengthened their local governments, businesses, and other associations to act on the problems. Occasionally an effective partnership between all these levels of interest emerges. But when federal monies are withdrawn from such programs, local interests have so little organized political and financial power that they simply stop building. Quite otherwise when a local defense industry is threatened with closing: Its parent corporation with good "contacts" in the Department of Defense springs to the rescue, probably with the aid of large nationally organized corporate groups with their own local backyards to protect.

Discrepancies between public opinion and public expenditures are largely the result of structures that bind and isolate economic and political decisions in this country. In 1976 taxpayers supported a federal bureaucracy which, in the face of world food crisis and world-wide danger of nuclear annihilation, expected to spend $104 billion in armaments in fiscal 1977 and $1.3 billion on the Food for Peace program.[8] The fact that the United States has an estimated 8,500 long-range nuclear missiles against the Soviet Union's 2,800, and that just 200 to 400 of these weapons could destroy a third of the Soviet population and three fourths of its industrial capacity, has little to do with national decisions about defense spending.[9] Defense industry means jobs and profit before it means annihilation of the Soviets.

Nor does the average American citizen influence the shape of the federal budget with his or her most tangible contribution to it: tax dollars. According to figures compiled by the Library of Congress Legislative Reference Service and released by Representative Les Aspin, the average tax contribution by each of 55 million American families to military-related programs of the Federal Government in fiscal 1976 was $2,485. This compares with $301 for health; $258 for education, manpower, and social services; and $107 for community and regional development.[10] This is not how most Americans *want* their taxes spent. Despite much official rhetorical concern with unemployment among the least affluent citizens of the land, little public attention gets directed toward the jobs that might be created by a government switch of investments from military to human-service industries. Recent plans to invest $50 billion in the construction of the B–1 bomber need to be discussed not only in terms of the relative military wisdom of the device but also in terms of the relative national need for health, urban transit, better housing, and the jobs which might be created for meeting those needs. In a day when "diversification" is a watchword for industrial survival, one might even speculate on how an aircraft corporation in Seattle and an auto manufacturer in Detroit might collaborate with government for delivering American cities from the curse of their exclusive dependence upon cars as people-movers. Such a problem could have a mighty effect on Detroit's unemployment rate—and the deterioration of its urban core. And what sort of support would such an imaginative plan receive for a government that dared to ask (1) ordinary citizens and (2) aircraft-auto employees their opinions about such a shift of resources?

2. This fragmentary analysis of the governmental budgeting process only partly explains why a potential political majority gives tacit assent to a process of tax dollar allocation that runs contrary to its own preferences. No neat answers emerge. But two clusters of reasons stare out from the data of our Urban Policy Study: *First, many people are disposed to avoid or suppress awareness of the discrepancy between public interest and public expenditures because it saves them from an immense burden of fear and anxiety.* When asked how they

think the federal-budget pie is divided between defense and human services, many of our respondents scaled their opinions in the direction of their preferences. Few had accurate knowledge of the discrepancy between the facts and their preferences.

Anxiety is unpleasant. We automatically avoid it unless our inner guidance system (our faith, our life story, our values) impels us to face and probe the situation that makes us anxious. (At times, in the reading of this book, have you suffered such anxiety—even hostility? Perhaps this suggests that such a book needs to be "handled" in a group.) Unfortunately, politics, religion, and education in America often connive unconsciously to make it easy for ordinary citizens to avoid the unpleasantness of clashes between facts and preferences. In this sense our information environment is impoverished. If the news on one television channel concentrates too regularly on unpleasant facts like dwindling supplies of oil or the 40 percent unemployment rate among black teen-agers in our cities, we flip to another channel. There we are relieved to find clips about firemen rescuing cats from trees and a bicyclist completing an around-the-world trip.

Our resistance to the "bad news" is further strengthened by that individualistic strain in Americans which resists impersonal talk about systems. We like individual action. Television journalists know the public prefers personal to impersonal news. Human interest stories are usually about odd, wicked, or virtuous personalities. Thus we prefer to understand the problems of a welfare system by observing a single family and then to generalize about the system as a whole from what we see in that family. Occasionally, newspeople may tell us that "half the people on welfare are children, and less than one in a hundred evidences a strong resistance to being gainfully employed." But television stations that send out information which clashes with the disposition of a majority of their viewers risk being turned off. Politicians face the same risk. Many rightly complain of their constituents' unwillingness to *hear* the bad news along with the good. Any politician who has studied the problems of energy resources will tell you privately that gasoline consumption in this country must soon decline. Yet what politician expects to make this moderately painful truth prominent in a campaign speech? Mass-media research told advertisers long ago that we all pay most careful attention to information that is consistent with our values.[11] The advertising industry plays tricks on us every day by observing this principle. Television tells us: "You are important, your role is important. Do everything you can to reinforce your importance by using the hairspray, beer, and skin lotion that will help you get involved!" Or: "Be patriotic, support America, buy a car, take out a loan!" Or: "Be proud of yourself: get off that excess fat with our reducing pills." The humor in this nonlogic mostly escapes us because it comes to us nimbly concealed. The reverse side of advertising is not humorous, but tragic. Virtually no one advertises the problems of the affluent society. Some products, like gas masks and reducing pills, would be unnecessary if we had less consuming tastes. Detroit auto workers might better be put to work on inner-city houses while we drive our cars for a longer time or less often. Thirteen percent of the population could adequately engage in industrial production while the rest of us invented jobs related to persons rather than things.[12]

Sheer information about the injustices and hurts of our fellow Americans is available in abundance in bookstores, libraries, universities, and educational television programs. *The most basic reason for the lack of political awareness in America is not the unavailability of information. Rather, it is the lack of a life story which motivates people to face the anxiety of coming to terms with their collective responsibility for attacking collective problems. Criticism therefore must fall on those persons and institutions which make the strongest claims to being concerned for our basic life commitments: first, upon the leaders and institutions of religion, and second, upon the leaders and institutions of education.* Both of these institutions have failed to provide a majority of their members with a social life story and the political skills for responding to questions like those posed by H. Richard Niebuhr at the end of his book, *Christ and Culture:*

> What will become of *us?* What is *our* whence and whither? What is the meaning—if meaning there is—in this whole march of mankind with which I am marching? . . . What is *our* guilt, *our* hope? . . . What must *we* do to be saved from villainy and vanity, emptiness and futility? How can *we* have a friendly God?[13]

Niebuhr italicized the first-person plural pronouns here. Over against Søren Kierkegaard, he believed that the human "existential problem, stated in despair or in faith, cannot be phrased simply in terms of 'I.' "[14] Americans have tended to agree with Kierkegaard rather than Niebuhr. We are inept at phrasing human questions in collective terms. No wonder that we are similarly inept at phrasing answers in collective terms. We are not as a people secure in a life story that enables us to bear the anxiety of the struggle to define and to shape a justly merciful economic and political order.

The historical and survey data lead inexorably to the conclusion that *we must trace this meaning-deficit in no small measure to the one-sided ethical influence of American churches.*

But there is a second side to the deficit of anxiety tolerance which we discovered in many of our North Carolina respondents. Not all of them suffered anxiety blocks to consciousness of society's more desperate ills. Some are well aware of the ills; *but they have fallen into the comforting cynicism of believing that they have no capacity to do anything about such massive problems.* These citizens, whose life story has made them aware of collective injustice, lack the interpersonal and organizational support that might turn them from mere awareness to action for political change. They lack the security of supportive friends with whom they can talk about what they know. Indeed they are among the most depressed people in all 900 of our respondents. Not only are they psychologically depressed, they may be physically ill as well. Some of the highest incidences of insomnia and stomach trouble can be found among persons who express a high level of ethical sensitivity but lack friends whom they can count on in time of personal need. Anxiety experienced alone leads easily to bitterness and depression; it can be fended off in the mind by apathy or cynicism. But anxiety experienced in a supportive community can be countered by other people's hope and ideas for problem response. For these ethically sensitive individualists, community is rare and cynicism is plentiful!

These same people experience a similar vacuum of strategies and tactics for action in the public arena. "Where would you turn to make common cause with like-minded people for achieving new policies on our society?" Many answer, "I don't know." Not only are they unaware that many of their neighbors share their concerns but also they have no strategy for transforming any widely felt public need into practical public act. *Information is not their need, but human relation-*

*ships for transmitting and exchanging information, for getting in
touch with action alternatives, and for developing practical political
solutions to practical political problems.*

Does the analysis ring true? Then the pragmatics below should
make some sense. If the analysis is faulty, then this is quite far enough
for you to read in this book!

POLITICAL HINTS TO PILGRIMS
ON THEIR WAY TO ETHICAL MATURITY

1. FANTASY ONE: The Political Value of Sunday School

During her several weeks in the hospital, Shirley Weatherford's
minister, Tom McGrath, came regularly to call upon her. Some days
after her return home, he called there too. With his encouragement,
the conversation was drifting back for the fourth or fifth time over
the traumatic events of her heart attack when Shirley remarked,
almost offhandedly to him, "You know, Tom, there's a lot of selfish-
ness in what I do to you as a *sick* Christian."

"I don't understand," he replied.

"Well," she said, "I caught myself *enjoying* this near-fatal illness
the other day. People whom you barely know tell you how grateful
they are for your continued existence. They write letters which show
how, underneath, all of us are afraid of dying but don't know how
to talk about that fear. All of this is a real ministry to me, and I feel
uplifted by it. But the other day I sensed the spiritual danger in it.
When you're classified as 'sick,' church people push certain levers in
themselves, and you're flooded by their exceptional concern. Ministers like you come to visit, are careful not to raise disturbing subjects,
treat me gently, and begin to tempt me with the splendid pleasures
of being sick! So I begin to understand hypochondriacs better, their
insatiable need for sympathy, and their crippled personhood. Do you
see what I'm getting at?"

"I'm beginning to."

"My real point is this: If the only thing I 'get' out of this terrible
illness is the uplift of sympathetic friends, many of them my fellow
church members, then I haven't gotten half enough of what I think

God may permit us to get from illness. I mean, there are so *many* people within ten miles of here who have gotten as sick as I and who never recovered. Either they didn't have that wonderful emergency squad, or they were too far from a hospital, or they didn't even have a telephone to call up anybody, or they lived all alone. I read in the newspaper last Friday that a child in Henry County died from tetanus because his parents didn't know the danger of rusty-nail wounds. What I'm saying to you, Tom, is that it's time we stopped talking about how near I came to dying and started talking about people who die every day in Georgia because they don't get the sort of medical care *I* got."

"If you really mean that," McGrath answered, "you might get in touch with Edgar Friedland. He's the county public health director. Why don't you go to see him when you feel able?"

So she did. And the results of her conversation with Dr. Friedland came spilling out one Sunday morning in, of all places, the Couples Class at her suburban Presbyterian church. The class had been studying the International Sunday School Lesson, and the topic was the second chapter of Philippians. In the midst of the discussion, Shirley said in somewhat troubled tones, "You know, I've been thinking a lot in recent weeks about what it means to 'empty yourself' and 'take the form of a servant.' So many people have served me in my illness that I have felt that I just couldn't go back to taking the services of medicine for granted. So I went to our county public health director the other day and I said—it was stupid, I guess— 'Doctor, I want to do something to help people like that little boy in Henry County who died from tetanus the other day.' He looked down at his desk a moment and then said to me: 'Mrs. Weatherford, it's the sort of concern I live with all the time. I'm glad you share it, and it's great of you to discover this concern as a result of your own illness. But the truth is that Henry County boy died because the white public health nurse down there is an amateur when it comes to working with black families. Two things might have saved his life: enough money in the county public health budget to support a black public nurse in that county, or enough reeducation of the present white nurse to keep her from being all that paternalistic to black people. Which of those problems do you have the gumption to work on? I guarantee that the first one will take a large public pressure group two to four years to solve with the county commissioners; and the second one may be impossible. Take your pick.' I went out of his office sorta put down a notch. I'm about as afraid of working for four years on the public health budget as I am of having another heart attack! What do you think I ought to do?"

End of Fantasy One. Some observations:

Pastor Tom McGrath shares a strength and a weakness with many of his colleagues in the Protestant church ministry. He doesn't really enjoy the illnesses of his parishioners, but he knows that sick-calling gives him a *feeling* of usefulness decidedly welcome amid the ambiguities of his professional existence. Ministers seem nearly useless in the eyes of so many of McGrath's contemporaries, even his contemporaries in Atlanta, Georgia. So he has to admit that Shirley Weatherford's aggressive suggestion that they should stop covering the five-week-old ground of her illness and move into the action implication of her experience took him by surprise. If he follows the psychological theory of Erik Erickson, however, he will recognize in Shirley's suggestion an echo of her own first steps, as a little girl perhaps, from passive to active experience of her own personhood. Activation has to be associated with the first significant advance in personal maturity, and, with ethical maturity as well. Among our respondents, those who saw their lives as drifting along under the control of external forces were the very people to evidence alienation, apathy, and racial prejudice. Shirley Weatherford long ago conquered any major tendencies of her own in this direction. That she should volunteer to open the door to the public health system demonstrates that. To his considerable credit, Tom McGrath pushes her through that door by giving her the name of someone inside that system. By doing so, McGrath performs what might be called a "ministry of personal activation." He provides opportunity structures that encourage people like Shirley to take an active role in shaping their individual and collective destinies. Instead of offering her the false comfort, "You're too sick to be worrying about all that now"; or the upper-class-oriented advice, "Why don't you just visit some people in our own local hospital?" he takes her at her word and invites her to visit

Dr. Friedland. He thereby urges her to a new level of self-validation and sense of personal meaning consistent with the Christian consciousness that they both share. Such self-validation, we found in our study, relates closely to people's sense of satisfying interpersonal relationships at home, among friends, and especially in their communities. *But one of the most surprising of all our findings was that people's general spirits, and their freedom from such psychosomatic complaints as insomnia and stomach trouble, are more clearly associated with a sense of political well-being than they are even with happiness at home or satisfaction with one's friends.*

True pastoral care, therefore, consists not only of showing personal concern for people but in providing them opportunity to make the most of their energy, imagination, and experience for forging meaningful relationships with people outside their familiar intimate circle. The opportunities that need to be created include not only structures like Sunday school classes and hospital auxiliaries but also structures of community politics. By a sure instinct, the person named Shirley Weatherford is deriving political as well as physical health from her recent experience of illness. She stands now on the lower rung of the ladder on whose topmost rung hangs the sign, "Change in Public Health Policy." She is only on the first rung, and we do not know how high on that ladder her resources will permit her to climb. Already she stands at a more mature level of political involvement, probably, than the majority in that Sunday school class. Already she exemplifies the restlessness of citizens who cannot be satisfied with voting as their single act of self-validation within the public arena.

However achieved, a ministry of personal activation to her will occur as her initiative gets explored, developed, redefined, and continually reevaluated from fresh angles. This process could eventually prove to be quite frustrating and unfulfilling. The politics of government or any other institution discourages personal activation if the participant is asked only to give episodic approval to a system through primitive expressions of pleasure, anger, or a decision merely not to desert the system. Personal political activation involves a two-way interchange between the person and the impact of his or her actions. The resulting sense of efficacy leads to more initiative. If the person finds the environment responsive, that experience in turn increases the person's sense of efficacy, and so on.

As things stand, we do not know if Shirley goes on to experience such a sense of expanding efficacy. Much depends, in fact, upon the actual response of that Sunday school class and other potential allies and antagonists in the fabric of her emerging relationship to the issues of health care in her life. Her situation at the moment illustrates the precarious, misleading nature of the simple advice to her minister, "Get her activated around an issue of human need in the public sphere." Not necessarily: Ministries of personal activation, essential in the pastoral care of individuals, are not in themselves sufficient even for the mere increase of sensitivity to the needs of strangers and the injustice from which some groups of people in the world suffer. We found that a sense of personal integrity, assurance, and individuation in American society frequently gets expressed in the quality of Open-mindedness combined with *low* levels of Commitment to Others. This suggests that it is perfectly possible to consider oneself an active, self-assured person, inwardly comfortable, in charge of one's own fate, without much concern for the fate of other people. Shirley seems to have passed beyond this stage of ethical immaturity; but now the first blush of her discovery of a new realm of social justice has passed too. The problems of public health care are bigger than she was counting on; but, significantly enough, she expresses her uncertainty and anxiety to the members of her Sunday school class. Instead of rushing off in a flurry of activistic zeal for adequate public health nursing programs, she confesses to a certain lack of self-assurance by leaning on the members of the class for advice, support, and possible correction. Already implicit in the situation are three dimensions of maturity, matched by three possible dimensions of the church's ministry. The three are related to one another as sides of a spinning triangle—any one of which may at any single moment be uppermost or the center of attention:

1. The expansion of *personal awareness* of new obligations for the achievement of a just and merciful society;
2. The development of interpersonal *group support* for the person's experience of anxiety and pain related to the new awareness;
3. The gathering of some *collective strength*—or political power

—necessary for the movement from awareness and support to political achievement.

Look for a moment at some of the interrelationships of all three sides of this ministry triangle:

1. *Personal activation.* First, the very development of ethical sensitivity requires interpersonal communication of sufficient depth and intimacy to evoke authentic experiences of the Pauline relational ethic of upbuilding and home-giving. That ethic, we remember, asserted the impossibility of any human being living in splendid isolation from fellowship, *koinonia,* with others. What Paul found in his relationship to the tiny urban churches of the Roman Empire, Dag Hammarskjöld was still finding in his experience that "without the humility and warmth which you have to develop in your relations to the few with whom you are personally involved, you will never be able to do anything for the many."[15] Self-assertion, both Paul and Hammarskjöld suggest, has to be tempered through the "yoke of human intimacy." Otherwise the most sincere concern for other people in theory can turn, in fact, into the dread commitment of the do-gooder to do good whether others like it or not. And yet, on the boundary between the small and larger human communities, persons remote from our intimate circle sometimes need that very circle to represent them, preliminarily, for our own learning of what it means to be their neighbors. In turn that intimate circle may also require that remote neighbor to deliver the circle from its natural human tendencies to exclusiveness. In a Shirley Weatherford, a mature member of the circle represents the stranger's needs inside the circle. For the moment she trusts the circle to treat those needs as tenderly as it has treated her own. The manuever is a risk; her Sunday school friends may lack the maturity to bear with her in her mixture of anxiety and hope regarding the needs of poor black families in Henry County. Most likely, a few members will bear it with her and others will reject it.

In a world that stamps hard on only too many young sprigs of ethical concern, two or three such persons are stronger for change than ten such persons might be in insulation from each other. (Jesus knew that! Matthew 18:20.) Conceived in this tough rather than romantic sense, social love rather than mere social knowledge finally converts personal activation into a dynamic moment in the human pilgrimage toward ethical maturity.

2. *Interpersonal activation.* The likely division of the Sunday school class into supporters and nonsupporters of this very pilgrimage, however, will emit a cautionary note to church leaders. Ministers know that the push toward personal social awareness needs to be helped along in tandem with interpersonal support. The orchestration of this combination calls for rare skills of ministry in every member of the church, ordained and nonordained alike. We have seen that, unless a person's experience of community develops commensurably with ethical awareness, the pains and anxiety of social sensitivity can be debilitating. The career of many social reformers, we know, is short. A frequent pattern for some crusaders is to win a few battles and then to quit the war. Even a John Calvin might have sustained his heroism in a more fruitful way if he had relaxed more often into the sustaining fellowship of friends who loved him enough to criticize, encourage, and laugh with him. In his capacity for hard-driving, disciplined concern for the social needs of Geneva, Calvin himself probably paid a price in what we have called open-mindedness.

Less mature Christians than Calvin, in fact, inhabit American churches in the form of those who have suppressed social anxiety by limiting their apparent demand for interpersonal support in the church and everywhere else. Such persons are likely to applaud efforts to keep religion out of politics and to limit the scope of the church's ministry to "personal" faith and ethics. Such applause has great utility in their psychic economy. If one narrows the concerns of "conscience" to issues that the individual alone can handle, one avoids the anxiety of facing questions which individuals alone cannot handle. For them and for all of us, some issues are not inwardly *thinkable* until they are socially *discussible.* The provision of safe room for discussion, the liberation of our narrow fearful ears for the hearing of a word of God for human society, constitutes an essential bit of ministry to us all. And here the bridge of Christian faith that binds people on different levels of maturity can be supremely important. However fearful some in the Sunday school class may be at the mention of medical and racial problems in that setting, the fact that

Shirley Weatherford mentions the problems in the double context of her own sickness and the study of Philippians cannot be dismissed casually by most people present. The example of one member in such a fellowship can begin a breakthrough for other members. "If Shirley, whom I know and like, can speak this way, might it not be safe for me as well? And if the Bible in which I believe calls for this sort of love, should I not give it a chance?"

To repeat, only in some matrix of shared expectations and reciprocal affirmation of basic intentions is it possible to remove the sting of suffering through a shared bearing of its reality, or, on the other hand, to celebrate the bringing into being of some new possibility which comes as the fruits of this common struggle. Such a group can be truly upbuilding and home-giving to people depressed with concern or weary with struggle. Such a group can invite its "weaker brothers and sisters" into the adventure of risking concern and struggle in the very face of possible depression and weariness. The spectrum from the personal to the interpersonal to the sociopolitical is potentially seamless; we are dealing with one human reality.

As any minister or church leader knows, the interpersonal ministries of the "oikodomic group" cannot be designated by neat rules of thumb. Persons are to be cared for, intimate relationships are to be nourished, the great public kingdom is to be served. The intersections of all three dimensions constitute the fundamental adventure. There are times when personal, institutional, and social peace needs the disturbance of anxiety if faith, hope, and love are to be released. At other times ideas or actions by some persons must be sharply challenged or pruned for the sake of their ultimate maturity; and there are yet other times for quiet support, for incubation of that which is too delicate to challenge. In terms ancient to the Biblical tradition, such groups will combine a spirit of moral judgment with the forgiveness of sins.

The existence of such groups already in the churches of America can be documented. As an illustration, one picks up the 1975 annual report of the Social Action Committee of the Madison Avenue Presbyterian Church in New York City. There we learn that this committee has sponsored study and action in the congregation at large on such diverse issues in contemporary America as "national health care, . . . the special problems of the United Farm Workers, . . . the elderly on the East Side, . . . Vietnamese refugees, and the (U.S. Senate) bill to codify criminal legislation." The committee has held a retreat for itself on "the theological background for social action." All the ingredients of personal, interpersonal, and public activation are apparently present in this subgroup of urban Presbyterians. A final paragraph in their 1975 report testifies rather vividly to this fact:

> The stated purpose of the Social Action Committee is to assist the congregation, individually and corporately, as we speak and act on the particular problems and crises of the times, maintaining the Church's prophetic voice and sharing in its ministry of reconciliation. Because the Committee does try to respond to the particular problems and crises of the time as these may be brought to us by church members, we are not infrequently of various minds. Whatever our outward accomplishments, the Committee's strength is clearest at these moments of tension. Though one or another may feel momentary impatience, we borrow forbearance and willingness to listen from the steadiness of others until the way becomes clearer for all. The ministry of reconciliation goes on within as well as without.[16]

The spirit that glimmers in such a "routine church report" has deep continuity with the church of the ages. What Augustine said of the fifth-century church could hardly be more authentically echoed in the interior fellowship of this modern Social Action Committee:

> Our very righteousness . . . is yet in this life of such a kind that it consists rather in the remission of sins than in the perfecting of virtues. Witness the prayer of the whole city of God in its pilgrim state, for it cries to God by the mouth of all its members, "Forgive us our debts as we forgive our debtors."[17]

Unlike some versions of T-groups and other therapy-centered groups, emotional openness, forbearance, and spontaneous expressiveness are prerequisites, not goals, of an "oikodomic group." Feelings must be released and understood, but as the precursors of healing, reconciliation, and renewal of group members for their mission in the world. Lust and anger become transformed into energies of love and ethical assertion, through a process that includes all those gifts of the Spirit, given to the church *corporately:* confession, forgiveness, and interpersonal security which liberates each individual for a life-style free of excessive self-reference. In this process can emerge that rare organizational phenomenon which Donald Michael has called "an error-embracing ethos," a social setting which identifies and graciously deals with the foibles and neuroses of its members. Since most institutional relationships in our society encourage participants to conceal their errors as long as possible, a church fellowship rooted in the forgiveness of sins has a unique role to play in the lives of all of us who weave in and out of various institutions. Among other things, the practice of forgiveness delivers the church from the evil of its own pretentiousness. Knowing how they are a part of the world's problems as well as potential problem-solvers equips the saints with a prerequisite of their ministry: the ability to stand beside, rather than over, other citizens of the Kingdom. And knowing that they belong to each other equips them with a reliable home base to venture forth from.[18]

3. *Political activation.* As we know from the Urban Policy Study, the mere intention to undertake the public ethical tasks of that Kingdom is not enough to facilitate ethical maturity among the members of a human fellowship. Intention without action may equal deepened cynicism or despair. Along with his parishioner Shirley, Tom McGrath seems close to discovering this third requirement for ministry: the nurturing of collective strength for public political efficacy. The essential nature of public activation for the health and salvation of souls doubtless remains a rather new thought for both of them, and for a majority of the members in their suburban Atlanta church. In other parts of that same city, however, there exist examples of southern Protestant churches which long ago discovered this ingredient of salvation in their concrete attempt to be the People of God in America. Those churches are composed largely of black people, whose experience in all three dimensions of ministry should be seen, not so much in connection with Americans like Shirley but in connection with Americans like Louella McCabe.

2. *FANTASY TWO: The Political Value of Sermons*

When she first heard that Elizabeth Colby's unemployment insurance had expired, Louella McCabe went down the street to see if her friend needed her help. "I don't know what on earth I can do now," said Elizabeth. "Three children, an empty refrigerator, and I'm not sure the welfare will feed us without two or three weeks of going back and forth from that office."

"Well," said Louella with a sigh, "at least you can feed those children on food stamps."

"But how about *tomorrow?* That's how soon I need a loaf of bread."

"Don't worry, honey; they've got a new rule that lets you get a week's worth of stamps without even paying for them. Our preacher said so last Sunday at church." Elizabeth looked relieved, but Louella thought to herself, "Suppose I hadn't come to visit, and three little children were hungry all this weekend."

She decided to mention it to Rev. Hudgins. "How many folks in Roxbury do you imagine, Reverend, don't know the helps available to them? You know Elizabeth Colby doesn't come to church very much. I'm just glad you said what you did last Sunday. Otherwise I wouldn't have known to help her either."

"H'm-m," said Hudgins thoughtfully. "Maybe we ought to do something about that." In preparation for next Sunday, he did something: He called on the town welfare office and got an up-to-date set of rules governing the federal food stamp program; he condensed some of the regulations to a mimeograph stencil for distribution to the congregation and community. Finally, he decided to preach on the text Matthew 6:33–34 and to give Louella McCabe the credit for some of what he wanted to say. He knew that she listened closely to his sermons.

The part she remembered best from that Sunday's sermon was what happened afterward. Toward the beginning, Rev. Hudgins had said: "I was born on a farm in southern Missouri, and I always thought that Jesus was absolutely right in telling us that our heavenly Father feeds birds and people with at least enough to get by on. Even during bad years our farm always had enough crop to feed us. But when I moved to the city I went through a time of thinking that Jesus didn't know what he was talking about. In the city you can just starve to death! Then I got educated, you might say, to the connection between that ancient land overflowing with milk and honey and the United States of America. We are in a land overflowing with milk and honey! I had to leave the farm because my father didn't need me to push that plow anymore. And now there are millions of acres of cropland in this country that nobody farms because they can't find a way to sell the food to hungry people in the cities. It's all a complicated problem, I hear; but Jesus is not being complicated when he says: 'Set your mind on God's kingdom and his justice before everything else, and all the rest will come to you as well.' If we had all the minds of all this country set on God and on his justice before everything else, we'd at least have food in every pantry in Roxbury!"

Toward the end he said: "The food stamp program is a step toward 'his justice' in the matter of getting food to people. I want to ask you to do two things: If you're too young to vote, I want you to help distribute three thousand copies of the food stamp rules to every house and apartment a mile around this church. If you're not a registered voter, I want you to get registered between now and October 1. If you are registered, I want you to meet our congressman here in this church next Saturday morning. I called him up last Monday, and he's willing to spend sixty minutes here to listen to what you have to say about the food stamp program. He's not on the Agriculture Committee, but he tells me that he doesn't want the City Hospital reporting a single case of undernourishment next year. I told him we'd work in this community to help that goal if he'd come down here and listen to us for just one hour. Don't say that you believe in 'God's justice before everything else' if you think getting your washing done next Saturday morning is more important than being right here!"

There was no doubt about Louella's being there. She was no public speaker, and she had never spoken face-to-face with a congressman before; but she knew what to talk about in that sixty-minute church and town meeting. "Mr. Congressman," she said, "there's too much food in this country to let a single person here have stomach pains in the morning. There's too much food to let one more child be born into this world with a brain that's not quite right. All my friends here know that I have my own tears to weep on this thing; but we don't have to cry over it anymore if the farmers and the congressmen and the community will work together to wipe those tears away from us all forever."

She felt like crying as she sat down, but this time from a little bit of hope.

Whoever writes a history of the American civil rights movement of 1955–1965 has to reckon with the role of the black church in the conditions that made that movement possible. Black Christians on this continent accepted their own version of the revivalism that invited converts to flee the troubles of earth for the peace of heaven. Yet the very organization of independent black churches after the Civil War constituted a sociopolitical rejection of pie-in-the-sky religion. Like their predecessors the earliest Christians, postbellum American blacks formed churches as their clearing of a time and a space subject to their control; once subject to their control, and once subject to the Bill of Rights of the American Constitution, they began to reap the political benefits inherent in governmental guarantees of "the free exercise of religion." The black church was a shelter under which personhood, family, and other ingredients of a free black identity could flourish. More clearly than any other American church group, perhaps, black churches of the past century embody the indispensably political function of religious faith in the face of a society that, like the Roman Empire, contradicts the faith at vital points.

The role of the church as a contradiction to all the forms of racism and poverty suffered by American blacks has been vividly expressed by James Cone in terms of his own experience in Bearden, Arkansas, as a member of the Macedonia African Methodist Episcopal Church:

> The same ethos flourished appropriately in the northern ghettos and the Jim Crow south after the end of institutional slavery. After being told six days of the week that they were nothings by the rulers of white society, on the Sabbath, the first day of the week, black people went to church in order to experience another definition of their humanity. Like Mary Magdalene at the tomb, looking for the body of Jesus, folks in Bearden went to Macedonia looking for the One who said, "I am the way, and the truth, and the life" (John 14:6 RSV). And like Mary, they were overjoyed to find him alive and present at Macedonia. That is why they shouted and prayed and why Reverend Hunter preached such fervent sermons, proclaiming Jesus' presence among them. Those six days of wheeling and dealing with white people always raised the anxious question of whether life was worth living. But when blacks went to church and

experienced the presence of Jesus' spirit among them, they realized that he bestowed a meaning upon their lives that could not be taken away by white folks.[19]

The truth of the Christian faith, says Cone in many places in his book, became plain to black people in relation to their social experience of oppression. The church was one place where liberation from oppression could be experienced emotionally, socially, and politically. The minister preached the gospel, and

> the truth of the story was dependent upon whether the people received the extra strength to go one more mile in their struggle to survive and whether they received the courage to strive one more time to right the wrongs in this world.[20]

Louella McCabe understands the church in such terms, and so does Rev. Hudgins. Residents of a northern urban ghetto, they have advanced considerably beyond their antebellum ancestors in the arts of "wheeling and dealing with white people." They are closer now than any historic generation of black Americans to becoming full participants in the political culture of the local, state, and national governments of the land. In no small measure they have "saving grace" experienced in the church to thank for this fact. Indeed, compared with the cautious entry into the politics of public health by Weatherford and McGrath in Atlanta, the prompt initiative on food stamps by McCabe and Hudgins in Boston is breathtaking. Stories not much different from these two could be told of equivalent pairs of white and black churches in Raleigh and Oak Park, Cincinnati and Los Angeles. In this respect, many of the lessons of our Urban Policy Study were long ago anticipated in the concrete life of America's black churches, which early became a major resource for their members' achievement of personal identity, social support, and political activation. In this respect, the truth of the American black church experience both echoes the experience of the first-century church and witnesses to the gospel truth in the twentieth.

3. *FANTASY THREE: Claiming the Media for Doing Justice*

Charles Najinsky flipped to the local news section of the town newspaper to find this advertisement staring out at him:

Fairmont Community College announces the opening of a Citizens'
Information Center for the use of persons interested in community issues
like the following:
  —effect of new industry on residential property values
  —zoning law and its effect on your neighborhood
  —improved municipal services: garbage, water, sewage
  —impact of unemployment on Fairmont
  —preservation of green space
  —air and water pollution
  —citizen desire to get acquainted with differing national culture
The Center has been financed on an experimental basis by a coalition of the college, the State of New Jersey, and three local religious bodies representing the Jewish, Protestant, and Roman Catholic faiths, A major aim of the Center is to put citizens interested
in similar problems in touch with each other. Call 988–2561 for
further information.

For at least five years Najinsky had watched the paint peeling in
his neighborhood. His wife had already suggested that they sell the
house before his retirement to avoid being caught here forever.
"Well," he said to himself, "let's give it a try." He called 988–2561.

"We're building a file of people in each residential section," said
the woman on the other end of the line. "When as many as six
persons express interest in a similar problem, we send a letter to them,
with all the names, addresses, and telephone numbers. Would you
like to register your name, address, and telephone number with us?"
Najinsky thought a moment: would the whole thing get to be a
hassle? "I guess so," he said dubiously. He put down the phone
wondering if anything would ever come of it.

More did come of it than he had expected. Seven names appeared
on the letter which arrived two weeks later. One of them was a casual
acquaintance from the box factory where he worked. Another he had
met one Sunday at Mass. The other five were strangers. But that very
night, one of the strangers called to ask him if his living room was
available for a get-together. "Sure," he said. "Let's make it Wednesday night."

Five men, four women, and three young children came. Most of
them lived in their own homes, but two families were renters, and

one of these was black. It was the first time a black couple had ever been in that living room—a fact that pushed Najinsky close to calling off the whole deal. But before the evening concluded, their mutual concern for the neighborhood won out. The nine adults agreed to divide into two groups, one to study zoning and industrialization laws, the other to conduct a telephone poll of residents of every street represented by some family in the initial group.

Only three months later, the results began to startle Najinsky and (what they came proudly to call) the "Fairmont Fair Deal Association." Forty homeowners and fifteen landlords had decided to paint their houses. A cooperative arrangement for the purchase of paint had been worked out at 40 percent of hardware store prices. A retired grocery store manager in the neighborhood had been enlisted as a mini information center for bulk purchases of several items such as grass seed, snow shovels, and roofing materials. In the meantime, largely through the help of the Citizens' Information Center, they discovered that zoning law permitted "medium industry" to locate in Fairmont and restricted all but a few neighborhoods to twelve-family apartment buildings. Builders were urging the county government to remove all restrictions on the size of apartment houses, and there was even talk of large purchases of current low-density residential tracts for this purpose.

"What we've got to decide," said Najinsky at an open meeting of the Association at the synagogue, "is whether we want this town to remain a place where you can get to know your neighbors." (His wife, Lola, said later to him with a laugh, "A year ago, Charlie, you didn't know any of the people at that meeting. You don't know anybody just by living in a place.") The upshot of the meeting was a series of delegations to the planning commission, the county board, and the president of a large residential construction company. In the midst of all this, a delegation from Foamcut, Inc., in the person of the latter's executive vice-president, paid a visit to the officers of the Fair Deal Association: "The Federal Government is financing the purchase of the area of the South Bronx in which our present factory is located. They expect to build an apartment complex and some office buildings there. We're thinking about moving to New Jersey, and to Fairmont in particular. We are committed, by the way, to bringing as many of our present workers with us as possible. Some of them are having their residences cleared away too. You should know that a hundred and fifty of our workers are black or Puerto Rican. I'm wondering if, as an Association, you'd work with us to be sure that they can be housed in this community."

"Well, I guess we'll think about it," said Najinsky. "We'd have to think a *lot* about it before we tell you." The comment led to adjournment of the meeting.

Actually, Najinsky felt that there wasn't much to think about. Just when they were beginning to develop some real stability and spirit in the community, outsiders wanted to push the place downhill again. He'd almost stopped thinking about it, when he was invited one Sunday after Mass into Father O'Malley's study. "You know, Charles," said O'Malley, "your work with the Association is something we all can be proud of. It's the one thing we've done in this parish with the Protestants and the Jews that really makes sense. But I have a problem for you to think about. I don't want an answer from you right now, but I want you to think about it. A social worker from the South Bronx came to see me this past week. Her name is Harrisene Little. She was brought up there, loves the people there, is doing some remarkable things to help them. She came to me out of concern for thirty men and women who work for Foamcut, and who want to continue working with the company if and when it moves to Fairmont. They can't commute from The Bronx, and they would like very much to walk to work. They can pay modest rents, and they could live in any of those twelve-family apartments which the builders are willing to put up here. Everybody knows what a bombed-out area the South Bronx is. This would be our chance to help bear the responsibility for improving the lives of the people who live there. Would you consider working in the Association to get the cooperation of people on this thing? The Association could easily become a tool for locking up this community against people different from ourselves. As a Christian I don't want that to happen. I hope you'll think very hard about it."

That was the only kind of thinking you could do about it: hard thinking. Riding home in his car, he grumbled to his wife: "This Association thing just gets me in deeper and deeper. I was beginning to enjoy living here, but I can see one big hassle coming out of it now. I wish that social worker would just stay in The Bronx. What business does she have coming all the way over to New Jersey to see O'Malley? This thing is getting out of hand. Why don't they leave us alone?" Lola Najinsky left his question hanging in the air.

The forces insulating citizens, institutions, and locales from each other in American urban society are legion. The modern city is a highly differentiated society, if nothing else. Its split-upness is more easily experienced than its integrity. All through this study we have insisted that religious faith yearns toward the integrity—the peace, the wholeness, the salvation—of persons and communities. The threat of modern urbanism to integrity in all senses is immense. Charles Najinsky has begun to experience a form of integrity renewal. As his path crosses that of Harrisene Little, he stands at a critical point: Will he expend his network of urban community and responsibility, or will he retreat into one of the differentiated ghettos which the metropolis itself makes only too possible?

The question is posed to him as part of a process which the churches of Fairmont initiated in concert with a local college and a state government. The institutional innovation—a Citizens' Information Center—has a growing number of examples in cities across the United States. Our Urban Policy Study strongly implies the need for some such innovation if all the potential members of the People of God are to have the opportunity of identifying themselves to one another and of expressing their identity politically. *Precisely within the split-up, multicentered life of urban society the People of God need a practical method for seeing and encountering one another and their community in all its shifting boundaries—from the locale to the metropolis to the very globe.* The theology of the church has always held that the People of God are not coincidental with the members of particular confessional churches. Some expressions of the ecumenical spirit in recent times proclaim visions of justice and mercy for the whole global village.[21] The size and complexity of the human neighborhood on all its levels demand comprehensive structures of church ministry.

By Biblical standards, such structures must open doors to at least two sorts of people: "religious" people who need to discover their political vocation, and "secular" people who need to attain or recover a religious vision. Neighborhood centers may be such structures, and the idea may be briefly described here in terms of its basic principles.[22]

The complaints of contemporary Americans about the inhuman "bigness" of urban life have a tradition as old as the Puritan New England settlements. More recent was Thomas Jefferson's image of democratic national politics as founded on a network of democratic locales. Does modern mass society make such a notion old-fashioned? Not necessarily. What Jefferson described for his largely rural society sounds not far removed from the potentials of The Bronx and Fairmont if one thinks of modern communications technology as workable on small as well as on large scales. Our technology potentially links the large and the small scales. Jefferson put his democratic vision thus:

> Those wards, called townships in New England, are vital principles of their governments, and have proved themselves the wisest inventions ever devised by the wit of man for the perfect exercise of self-government. *Each ward would be a small republic within itself and every man in the State would thus become an active member of the common government, transacting in person a great portion of its rights and duties.*
>
> *The affairs of the larger sections,* of counties, of States, and of the Union, not admitting personal transactions by the people, will be delegated to agents elected by themselves, and representation will thus be submitted where personal action becomes impracticable. Yet, over these representative organs, should they become corrupt and perverted, *the division into wards, constituting the people in their wards a regularly organized power, enables them by that organization to crush, regularly and peaceably, the usurpations of their unfaithful agents,* and rescues them from the dreadful necessity of doing it insurrectionally. In this way we shall be as republican as a large society can be and accrue the continuance of purity in our government by the salutary, peaceable, and regular control of the people.[23]

Here Jefferson clearly envisions the necessity of national and state government; but he insists that all large political structures should be grounded in local public spaces where citizens speak, take responsibility, manifest courage, and win distinction in ways beneficial to others. Such a political order invites the involvement of every person. It encourages mutual respect between citizens and (as the Urban Policy Study demonstrates empirically) provides a basis for self-respect as well. The early Christian church exemplified these features, and down through history the church has anticipated in other ways such a political philosophy. That secular politics should embody its own intercessory prayer "for all sorts and conditions" of human beings, the Christian church has every reason to hope. For the nourishing of such a political order and as one of their basic ministries, the church and the synagogue also have reason to support Citizens' Information Centers in the Fairmonts of this country. Such centers could render a richer variety of public service than the tame word "information" or the scare word "politics" may suggest. In neighborhood centers citizens can foster art, tell stories, perform drama, make movies, learn to use a portable television camera, encounter the culture of foreigners, listen to music, and hear unfamiliar political ideas in the company of other persons. Culture, the seedbed of politics, grows more authentically in quiet human fellowships than in a frantic commercial television studio. Should not the facility of a television camera be as available to ordinary citizens as the facility of a television receiver? Our local and world politics might be more imaginative and human if we engaged more regularly in sending as well as receiving messages in our urban-global communities. The economics of buying-and-selling have dominated the first generation of televiewing in the United States. With imagination, compassion, and sound political instinct, city churches might turn this medium toward more humane uses.

Any institution that supports such neighborhood centers must have a commitment to the community and not only to its own institutional survival. We know that *every* institution is vulnerable to the self-preoccupation syndrome! But given their own limited resources and energies, neither individual members nor the governing boards of churches should see such an idea as calling for large outlays of money and other expense. What our cities need most is innovation in organization. The institutional elements of more humane communities already exist in most American cities: Libraries, churches, colleges, and governments already have the requisite buildings, people, information, and other resources. Churches and synagogues stand in a peculiarly promising position as potential catalysts of new combinations of institutions: As a People of God they have every reason—Biblically speaking—to seek deliverance from the tyranny of particular institutional interests, including their own institutional interests.

An organizational device of the sort suggested here can help deliver any person or social group from the same tyranny. We cannot be sure how this stream in his biography will turn, but Charles Najinsky is beginning to experience just such deliverance. His trek toward community with his urban neighbors began with a specific interest of his own—the value of his house. This seems psychologically universal for most of us. Two fundamental principles for the construction of a citizens' information network peek out here: (1) It must be responsive to the particular conscious needs of the user, and (2) it must help the user place his or her need in the context of the needs of other citizens. Such an information network might be called "contextual."[24] If lopsidedly responsive on either of two such sides, the system will fail to express a Biblical—or oikodomic—political ethic: simultaneous service to persons and community.

On the one side, most of us neither expect nor desire to be equally well informed or equally active on all issues agitating our neighborhoods, our cities, our nation, or our world. Each of us needs the capacity to get more information on some issues than on others. How clogged the channels of information may be on any such issues can be tested if you ask yourself what three problems worry you most about your own city, and how you would get accurate and action-relevant information on those three problems within the next twenty-four hours. One wonders how long it took Harrisene Little to discover the link between the housing needs of thirty Bronx residents and the possible help of the Fairmont Fair Deal Association. The question required real research, and such research is often unavailable to citizens until long after it might do them concrete good. What good does it do to read in the paper one evening that the construction company has bought out half your block at bargain prices?

But faithfully and ethically speaking, a contextualized information system must be responsive not only to an individual citizen's need but must also relate that need to the need of others. Ordinarily we expect politicians to be "brokers" of the diverse, sometimes conflicting, sometimes overlapping, expressed needs of the public. One can imagine how frustrated the local politician may come to feel in the housing debate in Fairmont. If the Fair Deal Association fails to develop any common cause with its potential neighbors at Foamcut, and if the conflict becomes an issue in the next county election, candidates for office may be tempted to exploit a community conflict which might have been best solved in other, more human ways. *Public officials in Fairmont will have the opportunity to practice justice and mercy, the more just and merciful are their voting constituents.* Some problems beat on the doors of politicians because citizens have failed to engage themselves in those problems, not even to the extent of talking together about them. Citizens should do more talking together: That is one simple conclusion to which this study has led. More stringently put: *Every citizen in a democracy should have opportunity to express his or her selfhood in the public arena; but none should have opportunity to ignore the selfhood of other citizens.* If an information system is to nurture justice, it must serve a plurality of interests. It must help neighbors to hear what they desire to hear and also what they may not desire to hear. It must provide enough information about others to identify the real problems of their mutual relationships. And it must facilitate hope for the solution of those problems. In short, such a system will promote personal fulfillment, build community, and open person and community to as large an *oikoumenē* as they both can bear.

4. *FANTASY FOUR: Making Big Systems Bigger*

His disturbance over the total "fit" of his life impelled Philip Delaney to indulge himself in some continuing education. The bank was always urging its executives to keep up-to-date. The banking business he now felt he knew well enough. The *connections* of banking with cleaner water in the bay, less crime in the city, and more peace in the world—well, the business school summer courses just didn't cover it. So he decided to move the focus over to the liberal arts. The next three months of Wednesday nights found him listening to lectures on "The Future of Cities" at Berkeley.

The two final lectures were delivered by a scholar introduced as "the only man I know who is a Republican liberal, a former employee of the Nixon Administration in HEW, a university provost, married to a wife who is city planner, and afflicted with a sense of the basic injustices of American society." It was quite a combination, Philip agreed. The man's name was Paul Ransom.

The impression of the first lecture upon Philip got expressed in an invitation he was not used to extending to ivory-tower academics: "Would you be willing to come early enough next Wednesday to have dinner with me at the executive club?" What had struck him most about the first lecture was the remarkable insight of the man into the American need for both the return and the revision of its dreams. "People talk about the dangers of big government, but what worries me is the lumbering along of a *big anything* in pursuit of a *little dream.* Most of the organizations I have worked with—government, the university, even a corporation—stumble because they have more power than they know what to do with. At one point or another in the life of institutions and societies, the most practical question in the world is, 'What ultimate human good do we want to serve?' As Kurt Lewin put it, 'Nothing is so practical as a good theory.' Given a certain dream, the various levels of government in America might make good on their boast of being 'of the people.' Given a certain dream, we might insist that the city of San Francisco be content with its present level of wealth. Given a certain dream, the Department of Health, Education, and Welfare might get a larger proportion of the federal budget than the Department of Defense; given a certain dream, the 'socialism' some employees of large corporations now enjoy would get shared in the privileges which a rich society grants all of its members."

At their dinner atop the bank building, looking out on the bay, Delaney described to Ransom as succinctly as he could the faltering of his own dream since 1970. It had faltered, not collapsed. He still believed that "this country has a purpose to serve in world history," but he was no longer sure about the purpose; he was especially unsure that his bank had any central role in either defining or serving such a purpose. "What intrigues me most about your first lecture," he said intently, "is that 'wrong dream' you said you had soon after going to work for HEW. The hope in that dream, if I understand it, is a new sort of interdependence. We don't have to insulate all the keys to health, education, and welfare into the hands of relatively few experts, do we? We could build an *accessible* society, right?"

"Yes, I think so," said Ransom. "But it would take a sort of religious conversion of a lot of us to the notion that we are put here on this planet to be bothered by each other. I mean, we're such an individualistic lot. Most people came out to California to get away from other people. That's one reason our frustration is so great out here. There's nowhere else to go."

"And that's true for the individualism of nationalism too, isn't it?" said Philip. "We've got to consent now to be bothered by the Koreans, the Chinese, the Mexicans, and all the rest to be on the receiving end of their presence in the world. And that's hard for us."

"You couldn't be righter," said Ransom.

"But look," Philip hastened on, "as much as I enjoy—in a painful way—dreaming dreams with you, what I really want is your help in correcting dreams and systems simultaneously. I used to think that this bank, the largest in this country, was a magnificent *global* achievement; but both my experience and yours lead me to see that this building is just a splinter waving in the wind. If we were *really* big, we'd have our billions invested in making that bay cleaner and in projects that give us all the chance that *On the Beach* will never happen. If you won't consider it too pretentious, I want to know how a bank vice-president and a university provost could work together to make life safe for our grandchildren."

They both looked out over the Pacific. Ransom remembered a poem by Keats. He said slowly: "Well, I have some friends still at HEW, and a rather radical colleague in the economics department, and a good friend on the welfare rolls in Santa Cruz, and a plumber friend who lives next door. We all agree on one thing: we'd rather have the personal capacity for *love* than any other form of wealth we know. Which means that for the sake of love, we would be willing to put some limits on our self-aggrandizement."

"And—?" said Philip impatiently.

"And we are willing to commit ourselves to six or eight years of work on four particular systems: the tax system, to permit voters to participate in the process of building budget priorities; the welfare system, to make its services no more and no less human than the visit of middle-class people to any private doctor; the corporate stockholder system, to permit investors and customers some choice between higher and lower profits related to higher and lower social causes; and city government, to permit more decisions in neighborhoods and more understanding of their functional relations with other neighbors. Can you conceive of yourself spending eight years working on one of those four causes?"

"I think I can," said Philip drawing a long breath. "In business we don't plan eight years ahead. Just five, or three . . ."

"Our grandchildren, remember?" said Ransom with a smile.

"Ideas, emotions, fresh perspectives which lack an organized constituency fade and are blown away by the first shifts of the winds," says Max L. Stackhouse, echoing a maxim of his teacher, James Luther Adams: "By their groups shall you know them."[25] The careers of Philip Delaney and Paul Ransom are identified with many different groups, institutions, even countries. They are at a moment in their life when they are willing to claim: "You shall know them by their dreams." But they have no illusion that dreams have meaning for coming generations apart from the social carriers of those dreams. They are on the verge, apparently, of forming a new organization, a coalition, perhaps a new institution, for the reform of old ones. We have no clues to their expectations concerning religion and its institutions in America. But their fundamental concerns are religious; their scope of dreaming marks them with something of the maturity of the People of God; and if their dreams bear fruit, it will be partly because others among that People coalesce with them politically.

Even in its dim beginnings, their proposal for collaboration resembles the advice of Robert Bonthius to Christians that they seek always to involve themselves in "trying to change a structure or two among the systems of modern urban society."[26] He enumerates five categories of such systems: (1) "socialization systems," such as the family and schools, (2) "economic productive systems," such as business and industrial corporations, (3) "special care systems," such as prisons, medical care, and job-training programs for the poor, (4) "central government and legal systems," such as legislatures, courts, and administrative bureaucracies, and (5) "culturally creative systems," such as the arts and mass media. The selection of one or another of these areas of concern will vary according to the person, the historical moment, and other circumstance. Both choice and commitment receive shape and power from the dream. At the age of fifty, Philip Delaney is humble enough to believe that he has no final, finished grasp on the appropriate dream. He wants to learn and experiment with Ransom to refine the vision while working to effect its impact on institutions where the two of them have some power.

For their empowerment, such persons need the full range of encouragement which we have already identified here as the relationships required for ethical maturity: an array of personal, interpersonal, and public securities that match the array of hopes and fears which their lives now harbor. Whether they have more to contribute to the church, or the church has more to contribute to them, we cannot be sure. The Delaneys and Ransoms belong with the Weatherfords and McCabes in America. They belong to each other. Their mutual emerging consciousness of each other cannot be separated, in Christian perception, from the work of God's Spirit in the world of the twentieth century.

5. *NOT FANTASY BUT FACT: Global Justice: The Politics of Bread*

This book began with six characters in search of the City of God. One of them has found his way only too *in*frequently into these latter chapters: Luis Fernández. From the beginning we have centered our attention upon people who live in the cities of America. How difficult for Christians to remember—not only that Mexico is part of America —but also that all *non*-Americans are as much candidates for the People of God as any descendant of the Puritans. Why do we find it so hard to remember the hunger of the Fernández family as we write about hunger in the South Bronx and in Henry County? How far out can we extend the perimeters of our awareness and actively politicized love? The answer to this question lies in the future. The fact is, none of us knows how far toward the Heavenly City our own earthly faithfulness to God might take us. The life of a Pilgrim People is full of divine surprises.

We conclude, however, with a true rather than a fantasied paradigm of Christian discipleship on the perimeter. There on the inviting boundary between local, national, and global awareness, growing numbers of Christians find themselves standing today. These particular Christians live in Charlotte, North Carolina, where they are members of a scattering of Presbyterian churches. Two of them, during the early 1970's, participated in the growing concern of informed Americans for the problem of hunger among people scattered across the African Sahel, the floodplains of Bangladesh, and the hillsides north of Mexico City. In the spring of 1973, these two—both women—attended a denomination-wide consultation on the question of the church's responsibility for the food-related problems of Luis Fernández and his billions of kinspeople around the world. This meeting assembled a hundred "ordinary church members" and several dozen "experts" on world hunger, including a sizable proportion of persons from countries with hunger problems. Seen alone, this five-day meeting on a university campus was just one more church conference. In the case of two delegates[27] from Charlotte, however, it proved to be considerably more. One of them tells a story, in a letter written to us, that illustrates the possibility of attacking the consciousness barrier between local and world political activation by groups of religiously motivated, churchly organized, interpersonally supported, and globally oriented people. Whatever may be the shortcomings of the program described in this letter—however afflicted it may be with the American temptation to take too *much* responsibility for the problems of the world—such a letter embodies a hope basic to everything written in this book. Our time needs a growing company of human beings who will help one another to overcome the equally dangerous temptation of taking too *little* responsibility for those problems.

> Trying to recall "first causes" for our Haiti Project, we would have to go back to the Consultation on World Hunger and Development held in

Athens, Georgia, in 1973. Two of us attended that consultation and came away with an understanding of the dimensions of the hunger problem and a compelling sense of urgency to do something about it. We were members of the newly appointed Hunger Task Force of Mecklenburg Presbytery which was groping for ways to educate and sensitize local churches to hunger needs and to motivate them to action. The process was slow and the response minimal. Most people felt overwhelmed and immobilized by the enormity of the problem.

One effort of that Task Force was to review with Dr. James Cogswell, the national director of the Presbyterian Hunger Program, great hunger areas of the world and the commitment of various groups for service there. When he pinpointed Haiti as one of the neediest areas, the Task Force sent one of its members there in June, 1974, to survey needs and bring back recommendations for projects. In consultation with our national Division of International Mission, he compiled a "shopping list" of needs to be met by individuals, groups, and churches. Here, again, response was fragmentary.

Thinking that a single congregation with many resources might be a place to begin some significant action, Lib Harkey and I, with the approval of our session, sought to help our 2,400-member congregation recognize its latent potential for undertaking a project to address the root causes of hunger and serve as a model for other concerned congregations. A Myers Park Presbyterian Church Task Force was organized to explore possible courses of action. Realizing that a precursor to action is to be informed, we offered a study course in the causes and current status of the hunger problem, led by the faculty of Davidson College's Economics Department and the North Carolina–Virginia director of the Christian Rural Overseas Program.

Shortly after this, a group with similar concerns began to meet at Covenant Presbyterian Church, and soon we combined efforts and formed a joint committee. Two subgroups were designated to research possibilities for a local project and an international one. It was hoped that when the research was completed, the entire presbytery could be challenged to participate in supporting the proposed international project as an expression of Christian mission.

The international subgroup met on an average of once every 3 weeks for a year. Presbytery's executive attended these meetings. We considered hunger-affected countries, studied the characteristics and problems of developing countries, read a variety of materials from lengthy bibliographies, and discussed various facets of overseas work with furloughed missionaries and experts from such agencies as our national overseas mission board.

The first phase of study ended with the selection of Haiti as our target country. Its needs, its proximity, and our chances for success there were determining factors in its selection. We decided to undertake a long-range effort in integrated rural development in cooperation with Haitian Christians, working through existing Haitian institutions whenever possible, to stimulate the selected community to participate in solving its problems. We wanted Haitians to share in planning, directing, and implementing the project so that they could continue it themselves as we phased out.

With denominational funding, a 7-person team went to Haiti for 4 days in May, 1975. The team consisted of the Latin-American Area Secretary of the Division of International Mission (DIM), members from both churches, the chairman of presbytery's council, and an agricultural expert from North Carolina State University with experience in agricultural development in developing countries. This team met with Haitian church leaders, government officials, local community councils, private citizens, and heads of other agencies working in Haiti. They assured people of our interest and concern and asked how we might be of help. They were received with enthusiasm, and it was in response to needs expressed by the Haitians themselves that the team selected a site (not the worst or the best, but one with undeveloped potential), evaluated the credentials of a potential director, and outlined additional local information needed.

Two people were employed, with funds for their salaries coming through a grant from the Division, after the team's recommendations were endorsed back home. One was a seven-year resident of Haiti with a long record of success with Church World Service development programs, the other a Haitian sociologist. The wife of the former, a sociologist working on her Ph.D., was also hired on a per diem basis to help with research, proposal preparation, and evaluation.

With the resulting design in hand, the subcommittee drew up a proposal which was submitted to Mecklenburg Presbytery in November, 1975. It recommended that presbytery, through a Haiti Development Commission, undertake, in partnership with Haitian churches and the Division, a seven- to ten-year project aimed at alleviating the root of hunger in the Belladere–Croix Fer region of Haiti. The subcommittee recommended that the program be one of integrated development in cooperation with Christian churches and community councils in that area, with the following components: agriculture, public health, family planning, education, economic development, and transportation, funded through a three-year campaign for $800,000 initiated by presbytery.

Construction of an irrigation canal was chosen as the initial phase of the project. Local residents, working together, have completed seven sections, of twenty meters each, of the canal, with four more sections under way. Presbytery has given money to buy the simple tools needed for construction. An "animator" (on-the-scene organizer) has been hired and is awakening the people of Belladere–Croix Fer to the fact that they can do something to help themselves. A health assistant has also been employed. She is teaching a hygiene class and is gathering data about community health problems. Committees, or work groups, have been formed, and a structure for working with government agencies is being set up. For example, a food committee is providing the noon meal for peasants digging the canal; a rural youth group has started a *jardin* or community garden on land donated by a local farmer; a local carpenter is teaching the youth to repair their school furniture; and a health committee is collecting funds to buy medicine and material to build simple furniture for a medical clinic. Through discussions with the "animator," surrounding areas have been motivated to organize community councils.

See what the 1973 Hunger Program started? We think it's exciting!

For the record: Karl A. Ostrom and Donald W. Shriver, Jr., think that it's exciting, too. We think so, for reasons spread before you in this book. And we wish you, fellow citizens with God's people, "deep roots and firm foundations" in these reasons. To say it more exactly, we wish you what was wished for our spiritual antecedents in an ancient city. Like us, they were just learning to become a Pilgrim People:

> May you be strong to grasp, with all God's people, what is the breadth and length and height and depth of the love of Christ, and to know it, though it is beyond knowledge. So may you attain to fullness of being, the fullness of God himself.
>
> Now to him who is able to do immeasurably more than all we can ask or conceive, by the power which is at work among us, to him be glory in the church and in Christ Jesus from generation to generation evermore! (Eph. 3:18–21)

Notes

CHAPTER 1

AN ARRAY OF HOPES AND FEARS

1. Lewis Thomas, *The Lives of a Cell* (Bantam Books, Inc., 1974), pp. 52–53.

2. The names of three persons described here have been changed, but all three—Shirley Weatherford, Harrisene Little, and Paul Ransom—are actual persons. Harrisene Little's letter was first published in *The Nation*, May 20, 1968, and is printed in Leo Hamalian and Frederick R. Karl (eds.), *The Fourth World* (Dell Publishing Co., Inc., Laurel Books, 1976), pp. 154–159.

3. William Irwin Thompson, "What's past is prologue. The past —what's that?" *The New York Times*, June 10, 1976.

4. Eliezer Berkovits, *Faith After the Holocaust* (Ktav Publishing House, Inc., 1973), pp. 73–74. The quotation is from Albert Camus, *The Plague* (Alfred A. Knopf, Inc., 1948), p. 231.

5. Loren Eiseley, *The Unexpected Universe* (Harcourt, Brace and World, Inc., 1969), pp. 187–188.

CHAPTER 2

HEBREW HINTS TO CITY DWELLERS

1. The allusion to the Tower of Babel is from Genesis 11:4. One of the major studies of the evolution of city life in the world is Lewis Mumford, *The City in History: Its Origins, Its Transformations, and Its Prospects* (Harcourt, Brace and World, Inc., Harbinger Books 1961). Concerning the role of the early Middle Eastern kings in the establishment of the first cities, Mumford writes: "One of the attri-

butes of the ancient Egyptian god, Ptah, as revealed in a document derived from the third millennium B.C.—*that he founded cities*—is the special and all but universal function of kings. In the urban implosion, the king stands at the center: he is the popular magnet that draws to the heart of the city and brings under the control of the palace and temple all the new forces of civilization. Sometimes the king founded new cities; sometimes he transformed old country towns that had long been a-building, placing them under the authority of his governors: in either case his rule made a decisive change in their form and contents." (P. 35.) Readers seriously interested in the history of cities may want to consult this book.

2. Jean-François Steiner, *Treblinka*, tr. by Helen Weaver (The New American Library of World Literature, Inc., Signet Books, 1967).

3. *Ibid.*, p. 8, in the Preface by Simone de Beauvoir. For a comprehensive historical account of the "Jewish story" in the World War II period, cf. Lucy S. Dawidowicz, *The War Against the Jews, 1933–1945* (Holt, Rinehart & Winston, Inc., 1975).

4. A line from the script of the ABC-Television version of *Roots*, broadcast in January 1977.

5. All Biblical quotations in this book are from *The New English Bible* (London: Oxford University Press and Cambridge University Press, 1961 and 1970).

Two outstanding commentaries on the book of Jeremiah are the following: John Bright, *Jeremiah*, The Anchor Bible, Vol. 21 (Doubleday & Company, Inc., 1965), and Ernest Wilson Nicholson (ed.), *The Book of the Prophet Jeremiah*, The Cambridge Bible Commentary: New English Bible, 2 vols. (Cambridge: Cambridge University Press, 1973 and 1975).

6. W. B. Yeats, "The Second Coming," in *Modern Poetry* (Prentice-Hall, Inc., 1950), p. 65.

7. G. Ernest Wright, "The Faith of Israel," *The Interpreter's Bible* (Abingdon-Cokesbury Press, 1952), Vol. 1, p. 369. For another prophetic denunciation, full of the same linking of idolatry and social injustice to city life, see Micah, ch. 1, where that prophet indicts all the cities of the region.

8. The accent on economic abundance in Jeremiah's vision of the future is one illustration of George Ernest Wright's summary of the

Old Testament's theology and ethic for economic life: "Biblical man, especially in the Old Testament, set great value upon the good things of earth which God had provided for man's enjoyment. Hence economic life, which is the system of arrangements whereby these good things are secured and distributed, could no more be looked upon as evil in itself than could the goods themselves. Material abundance was seen as an evil in two situations only: *(a)* when it led members of the community to a denial of their dependence upon and obedience to their Lord; and *(b)* when it was gained at the expense and impoverishment of the weaker neighbor." (*The Biblical Doctrine of Man in Society,* p. 144; London: SCM Press, Ltd., 1954.)

9. Cf. Norman H. Snaith, *The Distinctive Ideas of the Old Testament* (Schocken Books, Inc., 1964), p. 120. The term for "righteousness" in the prophets, says Snaith, "is always toppling over into a preference for the poor and helpless."

10. Recent study of the formation of the Hebrew Bible tells us that the final "filtering" of what became our Old Testament took place in these synagogues of the diaspora. It was here that some of the writings of prophets and others were declared "sacred," and others were excluded. Thus, in the very editing of the book that finally became our Bible, there was presupposed the thesis of Jeremiah and other prophets that "we Jews must learn to live in the cities of the Gentiles, because our own city—Jerusalem—remains in great spiritual and political disrepair." Neither spiritually nor politically did Jerusalem ever really "return," as the prophets had hoped, in the centuries following the Exile. Only in Ezek., chs. 40 to 48, did a subsequent prophet suggest that Jerusalem in fact was having its glory restored. (We are indebted to Professor James Sanders for some of these observations.)

CHAPTER 3

"In Jerusalem . . . and to the Ends of the Earth"

1. Erich Auerbach, *Mimesis: The Representation of Reality in Western Literature,* tr. by Willard Trask (Doubleday & Company, Inc., Anchor Books, 1957).

2. Charles N. Cochrane makes much the same point in his com-

parison between Marcus Aurelius, the Stoic philosopher-emperor of
the second century A.D., and Augustine of Hippo, the Christian
bishop of the early fifth century. In the autobiographical *Meditations*
of Aurelius, "the shadow of the great man lies for ever across the
page," while in Augustine's *Confessions* the story is told of "a boy
born, not to the purple, but to a relatively humble station in life.
. . . The former is concerned never to expose a weakness, remembering that it is his business to exemplify so far as possible the conventional type of excellence enshrined in the heroic ideal. Accordingly,
the one produces a text-book of virtue . . . while the other achieved
a record so fresh and vivid as to have moved William James to
describe him as the 'first modern man'; the picture of a concrete
human being in whose presence the barriers of time and space drop
away to reveal him as one in all respects akin to ourselves; a being
so far unique in history, yet clothed with the common graces and
disgraces of mankind." And what epitomizes the differences between
the two books? "The work of Augustine was addressed to God, that
of Aurelius was addressed to himself." (Charles N. Cochrane, *Christianity and Classical Culture*, pp. 386–387; Oxford University Press,
Galaxy Books, 1957.) Any reader deeply interested in understanding
the revolutionary cultural transformation brought by Christian *thinking* to the ancient classical world will find this one of the best books
ever written on the subject.

3. Auerbach, *op. cit.*, pp. 36–38.

4. Cf. Cochrane, *op. cit.*, p. 26.

5. Paul L. Lehmann, "The Bible and the Significance of Civilization," *Theology Today*, Vol. V (1948), pp. 351–352, quoted by G.
Ernest Wright, *The Biblical Doctrine of Man in Society*, p. 166. The
notion of "specious ultimacy" Wright quotes from Paul Minear,
writing in the same issue of this journal, "The New Testament
Witness and Civilization," p. 345.

6. Quoted by T. R. Glover, *The Influence of Christ in the Ancient
World* (Cambridge: The University Press, 1929), p. 31.

7. *Ibid.*, p. 37. Though long out of print, this little book provides
in a brief way perspectives on "Christianity and classical culture"
which the Cochrane book (in note 2) explores in a more thorough
way. (We are indebted to Professor J. Louis Martyn, of Union Theo-

logical Seminary, New York City, for his help in reviewing this and other portions of this chapter.)

8. Cf. Cochrane, *op. cit.*, pp. 221–222. Cochrane consistently emphasizes both the social diversity and the revolutionary nature of the early church in intellectual, social, and spiritual terms. "The Christians, their numbers silently recruited from all ranks of society, constituted a focus for all who were in spiritual revolt against what they regarded as the barrenness and superficiality of dominant ideals." (*Ibid.*, p. 139.)

9. Cf. Günther Bornkamm, *Early Christian Experience*, tr. by Paul L. Hammer (London: SCM Press, Ltd., 1969), p. 126.

10. *Ibid.*, p. 152.

11. Cochrane, *op. cit.*, p. 512. Cf. also the summary of the reality and mutual reinforcement of "individuality" and "community," in the New Testament understanding of the church, by G. Ernest Wright, *The Biblical Doctrine of Man in Society*, p. 161.

12. As quoted by John T. McNeill, *A History of the Cure of Souls* (Harper & Brothers, Harper Torchbooks, 1951), p. 100.

CHAPTER 4

"A City Set on a Hill"

1. Again the most scholarly, readable account of these developments can be found in Cochrane, *Christianity and Classical Culture*, cited above, Ch. 3, note 2.

2. Augustine's classic, along with Mumford's *The City in History* (cited above, Ch. 2, note 1), would constitute hefty but valuable parallel reading for any Christian reading this volume. Cf. these two famous quotations, which summarize Augustine's theology and political theory: "Accordingly, two cities have been formed by two loves: the earthly by the love of self, even to the contempt of God; the heavenly by the love of God, even to the contempt of self. The former, in a word, glories in itself, the latter in the Lord. For the one seeks glory from men; but the greatest glory of the other is God, the witness of conscience. The one lifts up its head in its own glory; the other says to its God, 'Thou art my glory, and the lifter up of mine

head.' In the one, the princes and the nations it subdues are ruled by the love of ruling; in the other, the princes and the subjects serve one another in love, the latter obeying, while the former take thought for all." (XIV. 28.)

(And how shall we define a "people"—a political community?) "A people is an assemblage of reasonable beings bound together by a common agreement as to the objects of their love . . . then, in order to discover the character of any people, we have only to observe what they love." (XIX. 24.) (Augustine, *The City of God*, tr. by Marcus Dods, pp. 477, 706; Random House, Inc., The Modern Library, 1950.)

3. Cochrane, *op. cit.*, pp. 510, 512–513.

4. One of the now-standard historical accounts of this complex history is Ernst Troeltsch, *The Social Teaching of the Christian Churches*, tr. by Olive Wyon (London: George Allen & Unwin, Ltd., 1931). Fundamental to Troeltsch's understanding of the changing social thought of the church in history is his observation of the changing social position of the church in European society. A thousand years passed before the church's intellectual leaders began to claim that their faith led to the formulation of an ethic for the guidance of *all* major segments of the society. That such a comprehensive ethic "became possible in theory," observed Troeltsch, "can only be explained on the assumption that to some extent it must previously have become possible in fact" (Vol. I, p. 236). So successfully did the medieval church see its surrounding society as "Christianized," in fact, that it sometimes lost much sense of tension between "the two cities" of Augustine. "To the Early Church social reform was too difficult, to the Medieval Church it seemed superfluous." (Vol. I, p. 303.) Troeltsch finds an example, important for our perception of changing social patterns of cities, of the "fit" between medieval town life and the sense of mutual "care" which Christians were supposed to exercise toward all their neighbors, as follows:

"In contradistinction to the ancient Polis, in which aristocratic landowners lived together, which developed its own political and commercial policy, and educated its citizens on the basis of slave labor, . . . the medieval inland industrial town was a firmly established fellowship of labour and peace, in which a modest amount of property of equal value was held by the citizens. The medieval town, with its strong sense of solidarity, thus proved to be far better adapted to the spread of the Christian ethic than the ancient Polis.

"It was the city also which first produced that intensity and elasticity of intellectual life without which a vigorous development of the Christian world of thought is impossible; this is the reason why, from the very beginning, Christianity was a religion of the city. But the medieval industrial town was still very closely connected with the conditions of the simpler agrarian life; as a town of free labour and fellowship it was so far removed from the spirit of the ancient city-state that the ideal of a secular life controlled by the Christian ethic thus took root more easily in the town." (*Ibid.*, pp. 255–256.)

5. Among the books about John Calvin's life that might be consulted are these: John T. McNeill, *The History and Character of Calvinism* (Oxford University Press, 1954); Jean Cadier, *The Man God Mastered,* tr. by O. R. Johnston (Wm. B. Eerdmans Publishing Company, 1960); and André Biéler, *The Social Humanism of Calvin,* tr. by Paul T. Fuhrmann (John Knox Press, 1964).

6. Troeltsch saw the Calvinist movement as struggling to effect an impact on society more *total* than that attempted even by medieval Catholicism. "For the first time in the history of the Christian ethic —there came into existence a Christian Church whose social influence, as far as it was possible at that period, was completely comprehensive. . . . Calvinism was 'Christian Socialism' in the sense that it moulded in a corporate way the whole of life in the State and in Society, in the Family, and in the economic sphere, in public and in private, in accordance with Christian standards." (*Op. cit.,* Vol. II, p. 622.) Those standards, as Calvinists claimed, called for rigorous personal activity and equally rigorous association with others for the reformation of society as a whole. Everywhere the Calvinists went, Troeltsch observed, they formed "associations" for effecting social change, and everywhere they "laid down the principle that the Church ought to be interested in all sides of life" (*ibid.*, p. 602). The grand motive for all this activity, Calvin himself asserted again and again, was the "glory of God," and not merely the self-development

of human beings. As Troeltsch described the "peculiar combination of ideas" in Calvinism, it "produces a keen interest in politics, but not for the sake of the State; it produces active industry within the economic sphere, but not for the sake of wealth; it produces an eager social organization, but its aim is not material happiness; it produces unceasing labour, ever disciplining the senses, but none of this effort is for the sake of the object of all this industry. The one main controlling idea and purpose of this ethic is to glorify God, to produce the Holy Community, to attain that salvation which in election is held up as the aim; to this one idea all the other formal peculiarities of Calvinism are subordinate" (*ibid.*, p. 607).

7. Cf. Max Weber, *The Protestant Ethic and the Spirit of Capitalism*, tr. by Talcott Parsons (Charles Scribner's Sons, 1958).

8. McNeill, *The History and Character of Calvinism*, p. 190.

9. Quoted by John T. McNeill, *Makers of the Christian Tradition from Alfred the Great to Schleiermacher* (Harper & Row, Publishers, Inc., 1964), p. 194.

10. In a book that distinguished more rigorously than did Max Weber between early and late Calvinists, R. H. Tawney made it clear that in Geneva, "if Calvinism welcomed the world of business to its fold with an eagerness unknown before, it did so in the spirit of a conqueror organizing a new province, not of a suppliant arranging a compromise with a still powerful foe." Early Calvinism, said Tawney, "distrusted wealth . . . and, in the first flush of its youthful austerity, it did its best to make life unbearable for the rich." (*Religion and the Rise of Capitalism*, pp. 104, 115; The New American Library of World Literature, Inc., Mentor Books, 1947.)

11. McNeill, *Makers of the Christian Tradition*, p. 197.

12. "John Winthrop's Model of Charity," as quoted in H. Shelton Smith, Robert T. Handy, and Lefferts A. Loetscher, *American Christianity: An Historical Interpretation with Representative Documents* (Charles Scribner's Sons, 1960), Vol. I (1607–1820), pp. 100–102. All of the spelling and some of the punctuation of these quotations have been modernized. (We are indebted to Professor Handy for his review and suggestions for revision of various parts of this present chapter.)

13. Sam Bass Warner, *The Urban Wilderness* (Harper & Row, Publishers, Inc., 1972), pp. 7–8.

14. *Ibid.*

15. *Ibid.*, pp. 10–12.

16. *Ibid.*, p. 11.

17. Tawney, *op. cit.*, pp. 112–114.

18. Both of these quotations come from the Westward Expansion Museum of the National Park Service, St. Louis, Missouri.

19. The term "declension" was taken up by Perry Miller from Puritan writers themselves to describe the "fall" of subsequent generations of settlers from the original "New England Way." For further, searching study of the American Puritans, cf. Miller's two books, *The New England Mind: The Seventeenth Century* and *The New England Mind: From Colony to Province* (Harvard University Press, 1939 and 1953).

20. Adam Smith, *The Wealth of Nations* (University of Chicago, Great Books, 1952), p. vi.

21. *Ibid.*

22. On the whole of this history, eminently worth consulting is the readable, exhaustive yet interesting work of Sydney E. Ahlstrom, *A Religious History of the American People*, 2 vols. (Doubleday & Company, Inc., Image Books, 1975), especially Vol. I, Pts. III and IV.

23. Martin E. Marty, *Righteous Empire: The Protestant Experience in America* (The Dial Press, Inc., 1970), p. 69.

24. *Ibid.*, p. 108.

25. *Ibid.*, p. 110.

26. *Ibid.*, p. 150.

27. Quoted from *The Puritan Recorder*, Feb. 23, 1854, in Timothy L. Smith, *Revivalism and Social Reform: American Protestantism on the Eve of the Civil War* (Harper & Row, Publishers, Inc., Harper Torchbooks, 1965), p. 150.

28. *Ibid.*, p. 151.

29. *Ibid.*, pp. 154, 159.

30. *Ibid.*, p. 155.

31. *Ibid.*, p. 163.

32. *Ibid.*, pp. 174–175.

33. *Ibid.*, p. 215.

34. *Ibid.*, p. 235.

35. Robert T. Handy, *A Christian America: Protestant Hopes and Historical Realities* (Oxford University Press, 1971), p. 100.

36. *Ibid.*, p. 110.

37. Cf. Donald W. Dayton, *Discovering an Evangelical Heritage* (Harper & Row, Publishers, Inc., 1976), pp. 124–125.

38. *Ibid.*, p. 124.

39. Marty, *op. cit.*, p. 179.

40. Cf. Marty, *ibid.*, pp. 210ff., and Dean R. Hoge, *Division in the Protestant House* (The Westminster Press, 1976), pp. 24–29. Hoge's book documents this generalization on the basis of a careful survey of a sample of members of The United Presbyterian Church U.S.A.

41. Cf. the well-known book by Reinhold Niebuhr, which first brought him a wide reading audience, *Moral Man and Immoral Society* (Charles Scribner's Sons, 1932).

42. Quoted by Handy, *op. cit.*, pp. 211–212, from H. Richard Niebuhr, Wilhelm Pauck, and Francis P. Miller, *The Church Against the World* (Willett, Clark & Company, 1935), p. 102.

CHAPTER 5

AMERICAN CITY DWELLERS

1. Cf. above, Ch. 1, pp. 19–20.

2. Personal letter to the authors, September 1975.

3. Thomas Wolfe, *The Web and the Rock* (Grosset & Dunlap, Inc., Grosset's Universal Library, 1939), p. 223.

4. On this theme in primitive religions, cf. Mircea Eliade, *Cosmos and History: The Myth of the Eternal Return*, tr. by Willard Trask (Harper & Brothers, Harper Torchbooks, 1959).

5. Kenneth Underwood, *The Church, the University, and Social Policy: The Danforth Study of Campus Ministries*, 2 vols. (Wesleyan University Press, 1969), Vol. I, p. 215. Further analysis of what we mean here can be obtained from any one of a number of books growing out of a subfield of social science called the sociology of

knowledge. Among the two best books we know are Karl Mannheim, *Ideology and Utopia: An Introduction to the Sociology of Knowledge* (Harcourt, Brace and Company, Inc., 1936), and Peter Berger and Thomas Luckmann, *The Social Construction of Reality* (Doubleday & Company, Inc., Anchor Books, 1967). The "value theory" implied in this philosophical parenthesis is *relational;* and the best, brief, but difficult description of this theory we find in H. Richard Niebuhr's essay, "The Center of Value," in *Radical Monotheism and Western Culture* (Harper & Brothers, 1960), pp. 100–113.

6. Underwood, *op. cit.*, Vol. I, p. 195, quoting an unidentified poet.

7. Cf. Constant H. Jacquet, Jr. (ed.), *Yearbook of American and Canadian Churches*, 1976 (Abingdon Press, 1976), "Churchgoing Since '55," p. 256.

8. Since this is not a formal research report, we have made no effort in this volume to report at length the history, the design, the execution, and the findings of this study. Some five investigators formed the first year's researchers, faculty members of North Carolina State University and the University of North Carolina at Chapel Hill. The total research effort was funded by a grant from the Center for the Study of Metropolitan Problems of the National Institute of Mental Health, Department of Health, Education, and Welfare, Washington, D.C., grant #3-RO1-MH-19930. A full technical report on the project can be found in the forthcoming volume, *Which Way America? A Study of Community Activation*, by Karl A. Ostrom, Alden E. Lind, and Donald W. Shriver, Jr.

9. Weber's comment is from his essay, "Science as a Vocation," Hans H. Gerth and C. Wright Mills (eds.), *From Max Weber: Essays in Sociology* (Oxford University Press, Galaxy Books, 1958), p. 138.

10. "Like pure religion, pure science seems to care for 'widows and orphans'—for bereaved and abandoned facts, for processes and experiences that have lost meaning because they did not fit into an accepted framework of interpretation." (H. Richard Niebuhr, "Radical Faith and Western Science," in *Radical Monotheism and Western Culture*, p. 87; Harper & Brothers, 1960.)

11. John R. Earle, Dean D. Knudsen, and Donald W. Shriver, Jr., *Spindles and Spires: A Restudy of Religion and Social Change in*

Gastonia (John Knox Press, 1976), pp. 346–347.

12. Cf. above, pp. 50–54.

13. Cf. Charles Y. Glock and Rodney Stark, *Christian Beliefs and Anti-Semitism* (Harper & Row, Publishers, Inc., 1966), and (a significantly different point of view) Thomas C. Campbell and Yoshio Fukuyama, *The Fragmented Layman* (United Church Press, 1970). For a convenient review of sociological literature on this theme, cf. Richard L. Gorsuch and Daniel Aleshire, "Christian Faith and Ethnic Prejudice: A Review and Interpretation of Research," *Journal for the Scientific Study of Religion*, Vol. XIII (September 1974), pp. 281–307.

CHAPTER 6

BECOMING ETHICALLY MATURE

1. Weber, "Politics as a Vocation," in Gerth and Mills (eds.), *From Max Weber: Essays in Sociology* p. 128.

2. Richard Rabkin, "Evil as a Social Process: The My Lai Massacre," in Clifford J. Sager and Helen Singer Kaplan (eds.), *Progress in Group and Family Therapy* (Brunner/Mazel, Inc., 1972), pp. 792–800.

3. Cf. *New Voices in the American Theatre* (Modern Library, Inc., 1955), pp. 111–226.

4. On the difficulty of this combination for the minds of many Americans, cf. Robert N. Bellah, *The Broken Covenant: American Civil Religion in Time of Trial* (The Seabury Press, Crossroad Books, 1975), especially Ch. 5, "The American Taboo on Socialism," pp. 112–138.

5. Cf. Franklin H. Littell, *From State Church to Pluralism* (Doubleday & Company, Inc., Anchor Books, 1962), pp. 125ff.

6. Theodore Roosevelt, quoted in Marty, *Righteous Empire*, p. 12.

7. Gardner Spring, pastor of the Brick Presbyterian Church in New York City, as quoted in Robert T. Handy, "The American Messianic Consciousness: The Concept of the Chosen People and Manifest Destiny," *Review and Exposition*, Vol. LXXIII, No. 1

(Winter 1976), p. 53, from Spring's book, *The Glory of Christ* (New York: J. W. Dodd, 1854), p. 209.

8. Dwight McDonald, "Our Invisible Poor," reprinted from *The New Yorker* as a pamphlet by Sydney Hillman Foundation, 1963.

9. Cf. Erikson, *Childhood and Society* (1950), *Young Man Luther* (1958), and *Identity: Youth and Crisis* (1968), all published by W. W. Norton & Company, Inc.

10. William Glasser, *The Identity Society* (Harper & Row, Publishers, Inc., 1972), p. 72.

11. Patrick Conover, "Communes and Intentional Communities." Unpublished mimeograph, December 1974. Conover teaches at the University of North Carolina at Greensboro.

12. Cf. Bellah, *op. cit.*, p. 133.

13. Cf. Ahlstrom, *A Religious History of the American People*, Vol. II, Pt. IX, Ch. 63, pp. 559–620.

14. Marty, *op. cit.*, p. 12.

15. Cf. *Five Thousand Best Sermon Illustrations* (no copyright date; about 1920), p. 742. This volume is a valuable historical index to subjects and viewpoints deemed "popular," presumably by a cross section of American ministers of the era.

16. Terrence McCarthy, "The Last Christmas in America," *Ramparts*, December 1974–January 1975 (Noah's Ark, Inc., 1975), p. 50.

17. *Ibid.*

18. Cf. Jacquet (ed.), *Yearbook of American and Canadian Churches*, 1976, p. 245.

19. McCarthy, *loc. cit.*, p. 52.

20. "Why Poverty," *The New Internationalist*, No. 22 (Oxon: Devopress Ltd., 1974), p. 27.

21. Geoffrey Barraclough, "The Great World Crisis I," *The New York Review of Books*, Vol. XXI, No. 21822 (Whitney Ellsworth, 1975), p. 22.

22. *A Time to Choose: America's Energy Future*, Energy Policy Project of the Ford Foundation, quoted by Barraclough, *loc. cit.*, p. 22.

23. "The World Food and Energy Crisis," a report by Richard N. Gardner, cosponsored by the Institute on Men and Science, Rensselaerville, New York: The Aspen Institute for Humanistic Studies;

and others; quoted by Barraclough, *loc. cit.*, p. 22.

24. Barraclough, *loc. cit.*, p. 22.

25. William Serrin, "Detroit: A Midsummer's Nightmare," *The New York Times*, Aug. 25, 1976, p. 35.

26. Bellah, *op. cit.*, p. 134.

27. Advertisement, "Observations," The Mobil Oil Company, *The New York Times*, Aug. 22, 1976.

28. Walker Percy, *Love in the Ruins* (Dell Publishing Co., Inc., 1972), pp. 3–4.

29. *Ibid.*, p. 109.

30. *Ibid.*, p. 173.

31. *Ibid.*, p. 118.

CHAPTER 7

THE PEOPLE OF GOD IN URBAN AMERICA

1. Cf. John K. Galbraith, *Economics and the Public Purpose* (The New American Library, Inc., Signet Books, 1975).

2. *Ibid.*, p. 138.

3. Tom Wicker, *The New York Times*, Oct. 19, 1976.

4. Galbraith, *op. cit.*, p. 139.

5. Max L. Stackhouse, *The Ethics of Necropolis: An Essay on the Military-Industrial Complex and the Quest for a Just Peace* (Beacon Press, Inc., 1971), pp. 70–71.

6. Cf. Joseph Bensman and Arthur J. Vidich, *The New American Society: The Revolution of the Middle Class* (The New York Times Co., Quadrangle Books, 1971), pp. 11ff.

7. *The New York Times*, Aug. 27, 1974, pp. 1–2.

8. Andrew Young, M.C., writing accompanying letter to *Sane World Newsletter*, Vol. 14, No. 4 (Washington, D.C.: Sane, 1975).

9. *Ibid.*

10. *Sane World*, Vol. 14, No. 4 (Washington, D.C.: Sane, 1975), p. 1.

11. Bernard Berelson and Gary A. Steiner, *Human Behavior* (Harcourt, Brace and World, Inc., 1964), pp. 529ff.

12. Roderic Gorney, *The Human Agenda* (Bantam Books, Inc., 1973), pp. 390–400.

13. H. Richard Niebuhr, *Christ and Culture* (Harper & Brothers, 1956), pp. 243–244.

14. *Ibid.*, p. 243.

15. Dag Hammarskjöld, *Markings*, tr. by Leif Sjöberg and W. H. Auden (Alfred A. Knopf, Inc., 1964), p. 133.

16. Betty Haynes, acting chairman, as reported in *The Madison Avenue Presbyterian: Annual Report*, Vol. 38, No. 1 (February 1976), p. 17.

17. Augustine, *The City of God*, XIX. 27; The Modern Library edition, p. 708.

18. Emile Durkheim speaks of the "liberating dependence" provided by intimate primary groups that mediate between individuals and the larger society. Cf. Emile Durkheim, *Selected Writings*, tr. and ed. by Anthony Giddens (London: Cambridge University Press, 1972), p. 113. (For this reference we are indebted to Anthony Robinson of Union Theological Seminary and to his Master of Divinity thesis "A Small Church and Social Change.") Cf. also Shriver, Earle, and Knudsen, *Spindles and Spires*, pp. 308–312, on an issue often neglected in the study of the social function of the church—the doctrine of the forgiveness of sins and its significance for social healing.

19. James Cone, *The God of the Oppressed* (The Seabury Press, Inc., 1975), pp. 12–13.

20. *Ibid.*, p. 50.

21. On the pertinence of modern urban structures for the definition of ecumenical church structures, cf. Max L. Stackhouse, *Ethics and the Urban Ethos* (Beacon Press, Inc., 1974), Ch. 7.

22. For a more complete description of the ideas to be sketched here, cf. the larger research report volume *Which Way America?* by Karl A. Ostrom, Alden E. Lind, and Donald W. Shriver, Jr., cited above, Ch. 5, note 8.

23. Thomas Jefferson, "The Roots of Democracy," a letter to Samuel Kercheval, 1816, reprinted in *The Annals of America*, Vol. 4 (Encyclopaedia Britannica, Inc., 1968), pp. 422–426.

24. For a broad, thorough analysis of the interplay of information,

social organization, and political decision-making, cf. Amitai Etzioni, *The Active Society: A Theory of Societal and Political Processes* (The Free Press, 1968), especially Chs. 7 and 8, pp. 155–196.

25. Stackhouse, *Ethics and the Urban Ethos*, p. 150. Cf. J. L. Adams, "The Indispensable Discipline of Social Responsibility," *Journal of the Liberal Ministry*, Vol. VI, No. 2 (Spring 1966), p. 86.

26. Robert H. Bonthius, "Pastoral Care for Structures—As Well as Persons," *Pastoral Psychology*, Vol. 18, No. 174 (May 1967), pp. 10–19.

27. Ms. Elizabeth Harkey, mentioned in the letter below, and Ms. Danny Verner, its author.

Index
of Subjects

Index
of Biblical References